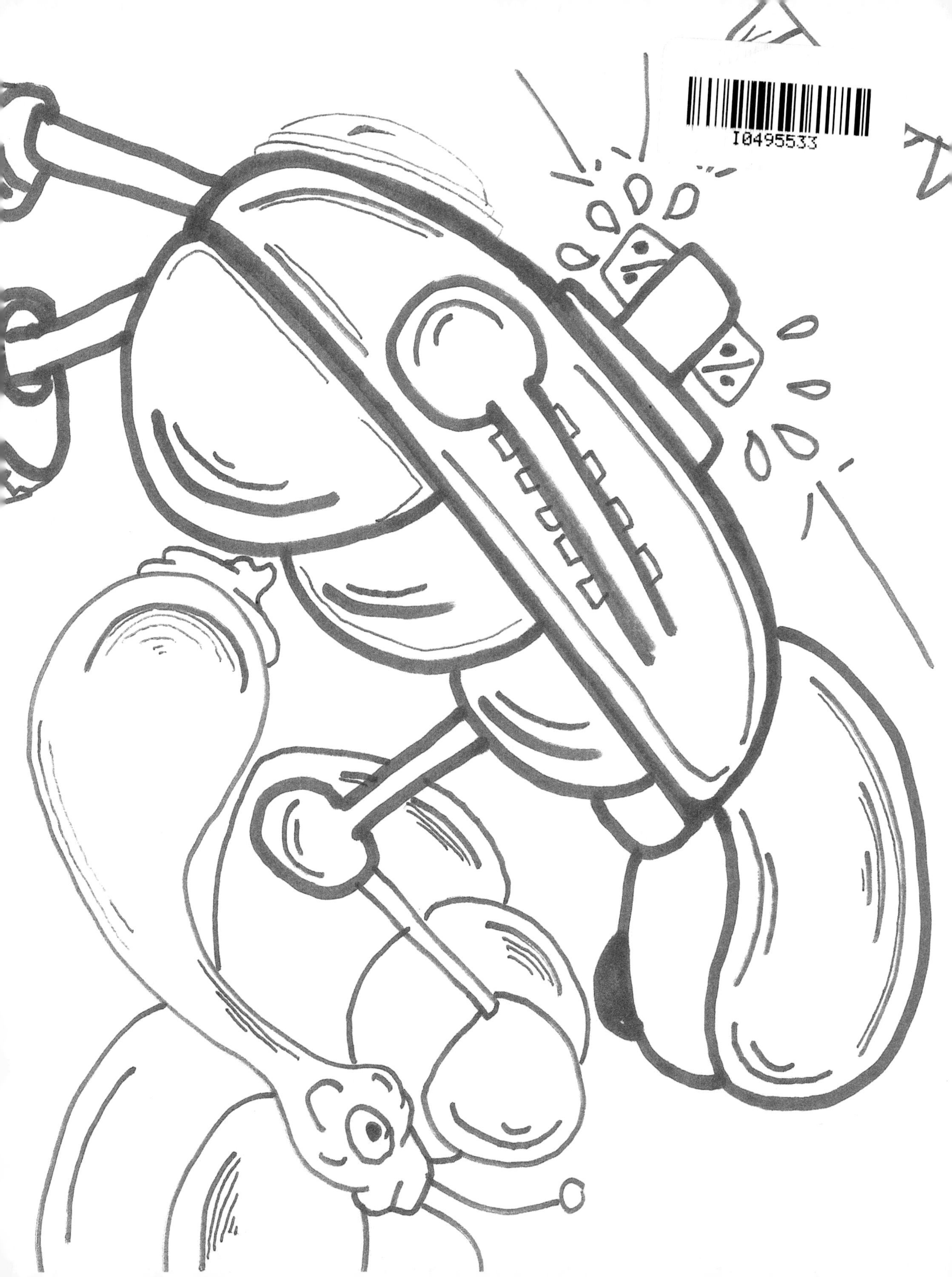

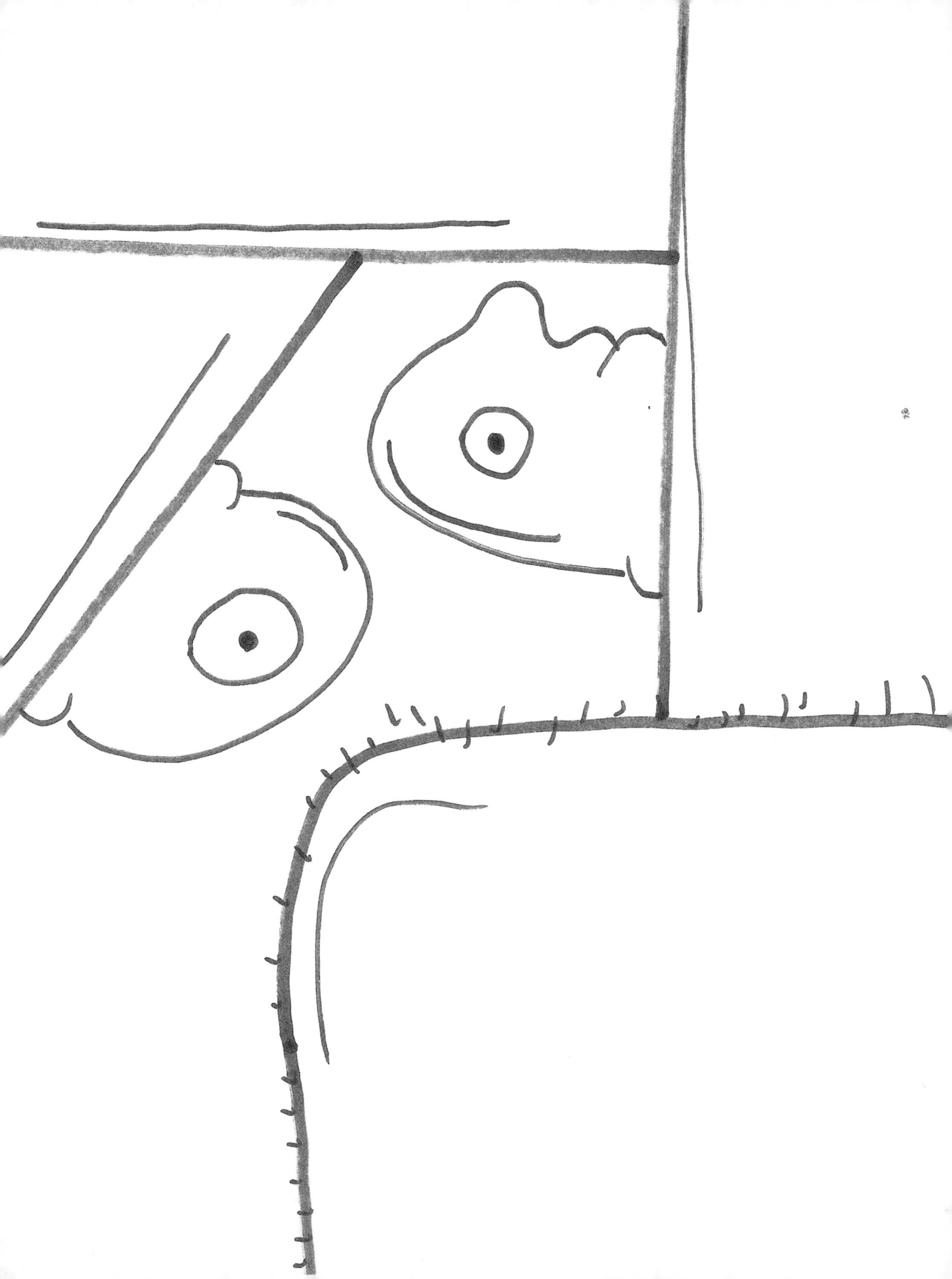

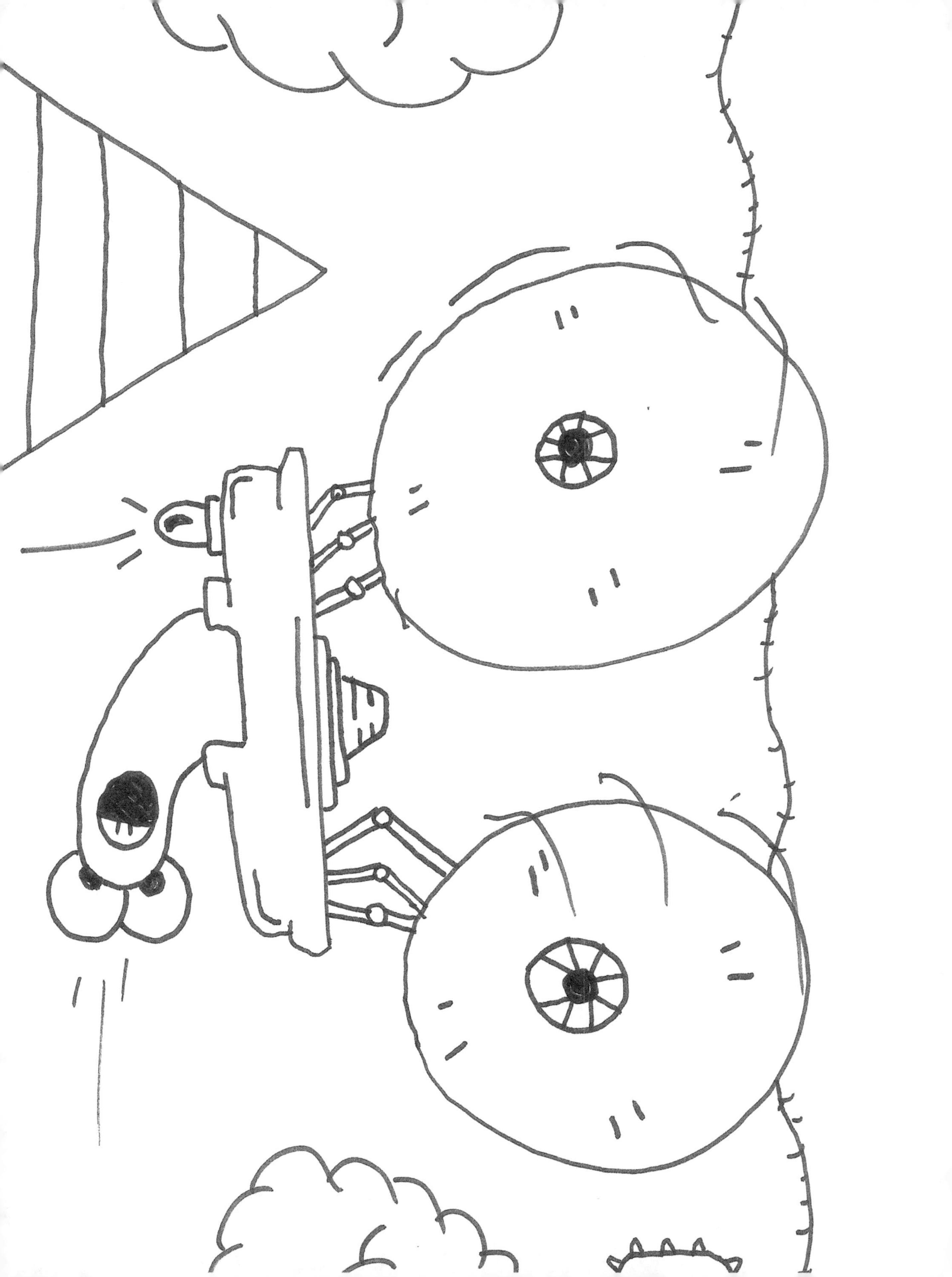

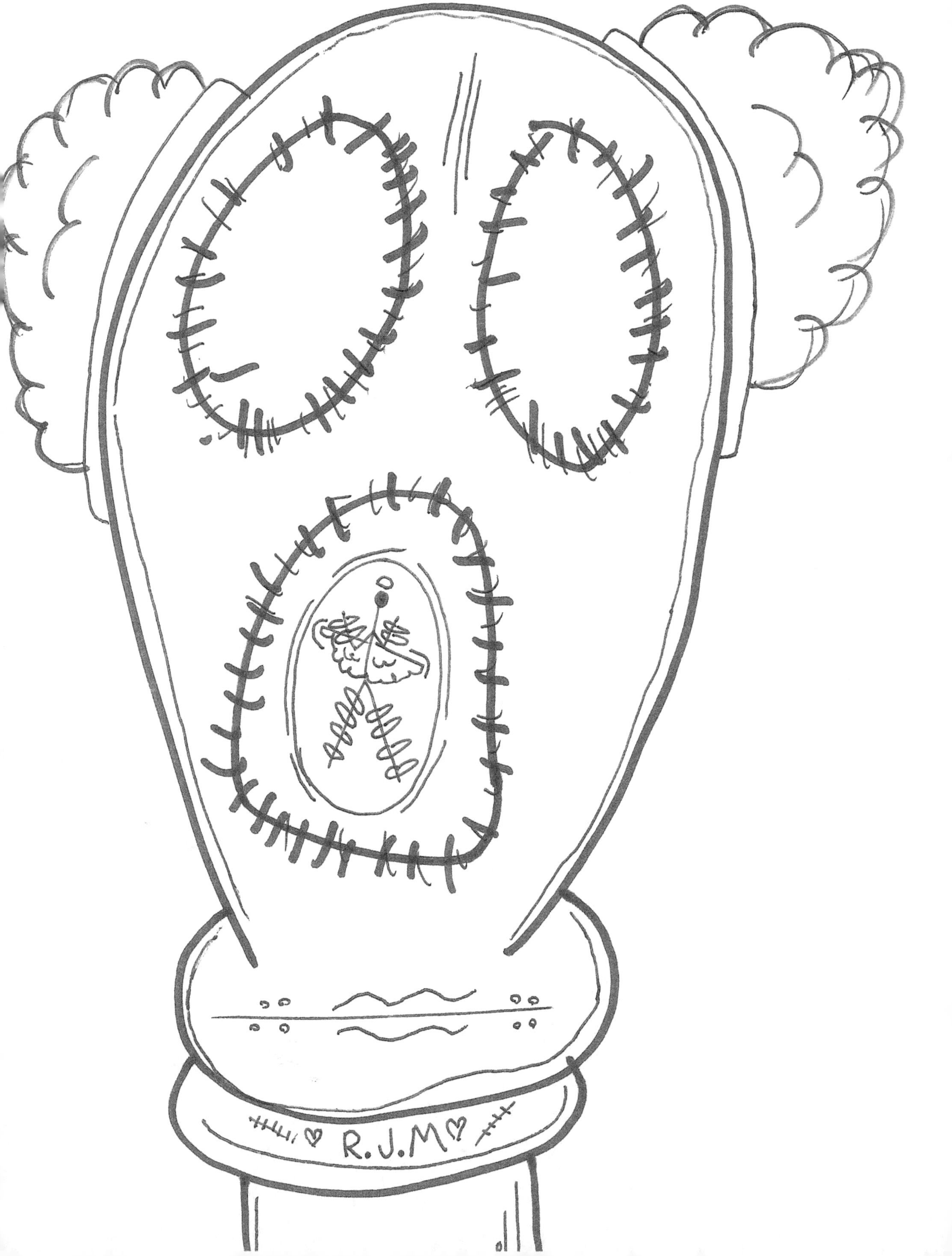
R.J.M

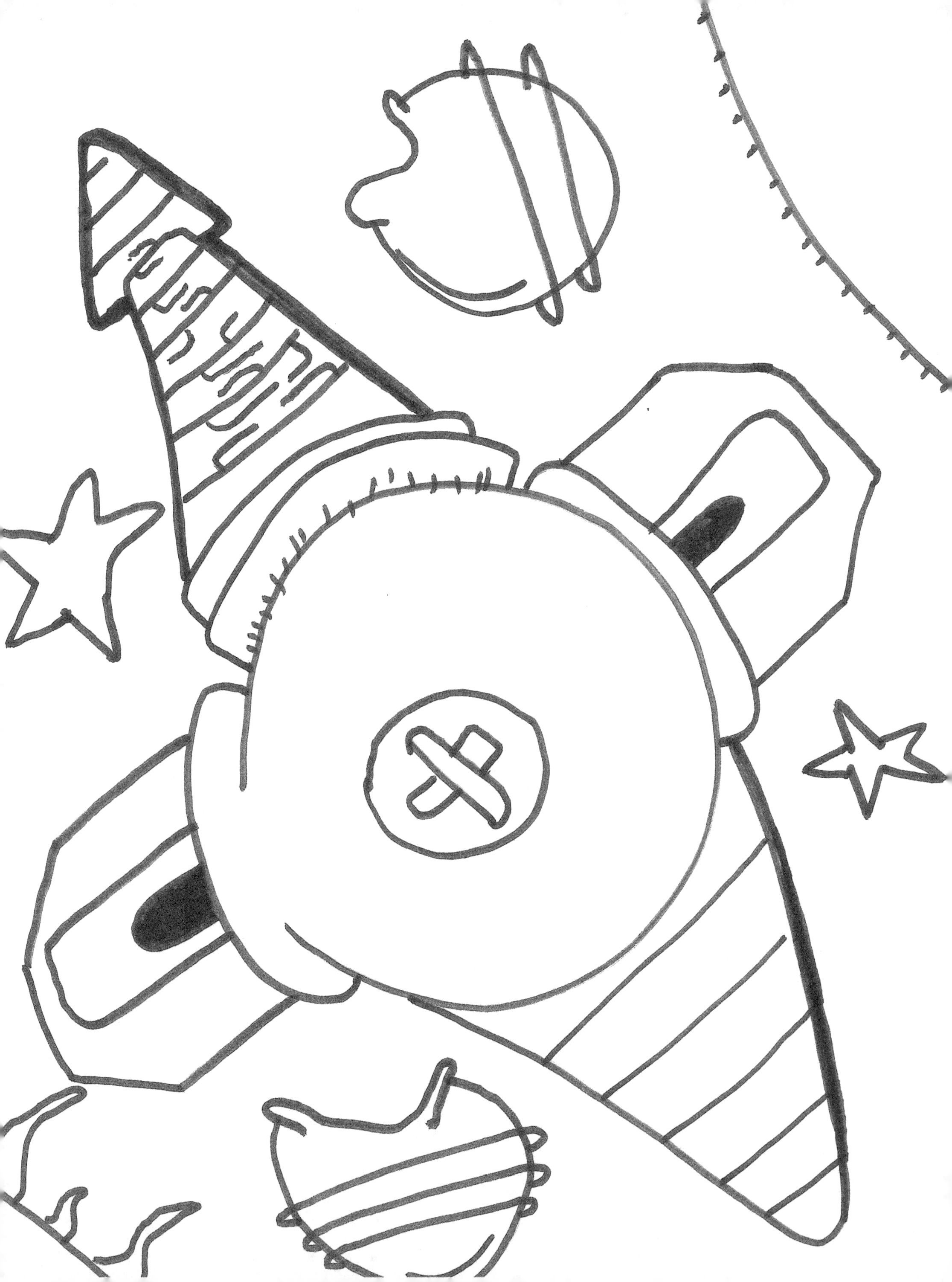

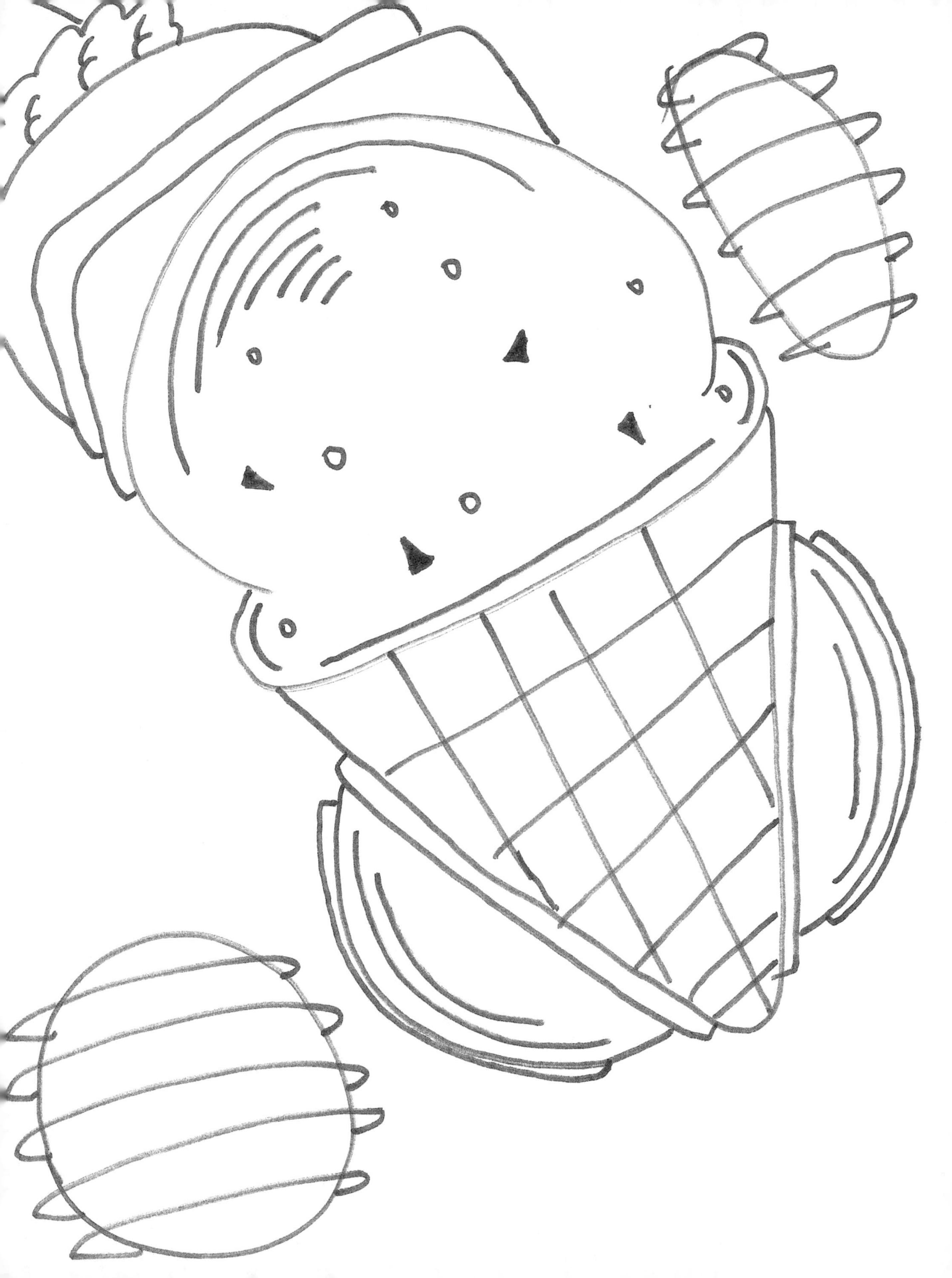

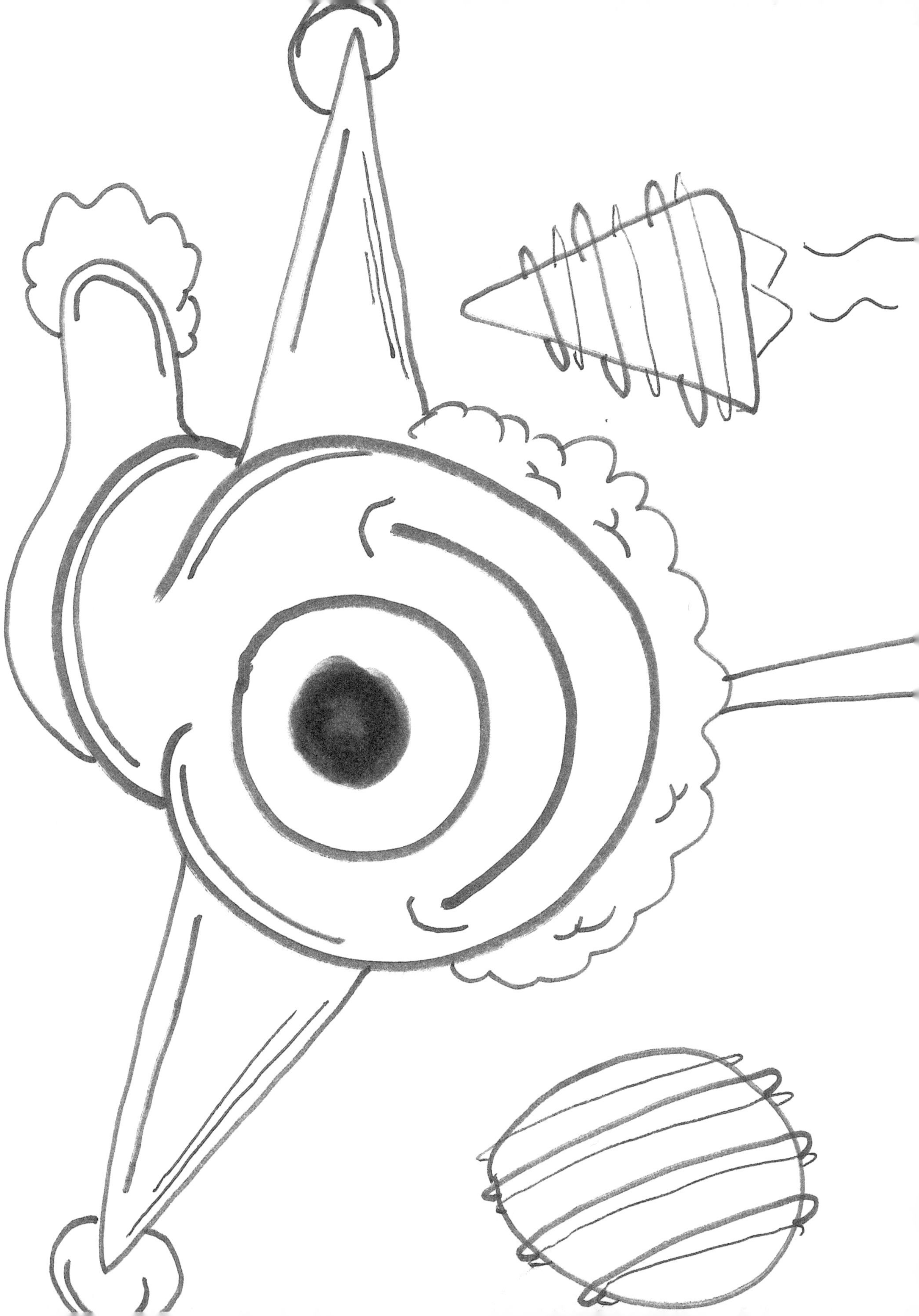

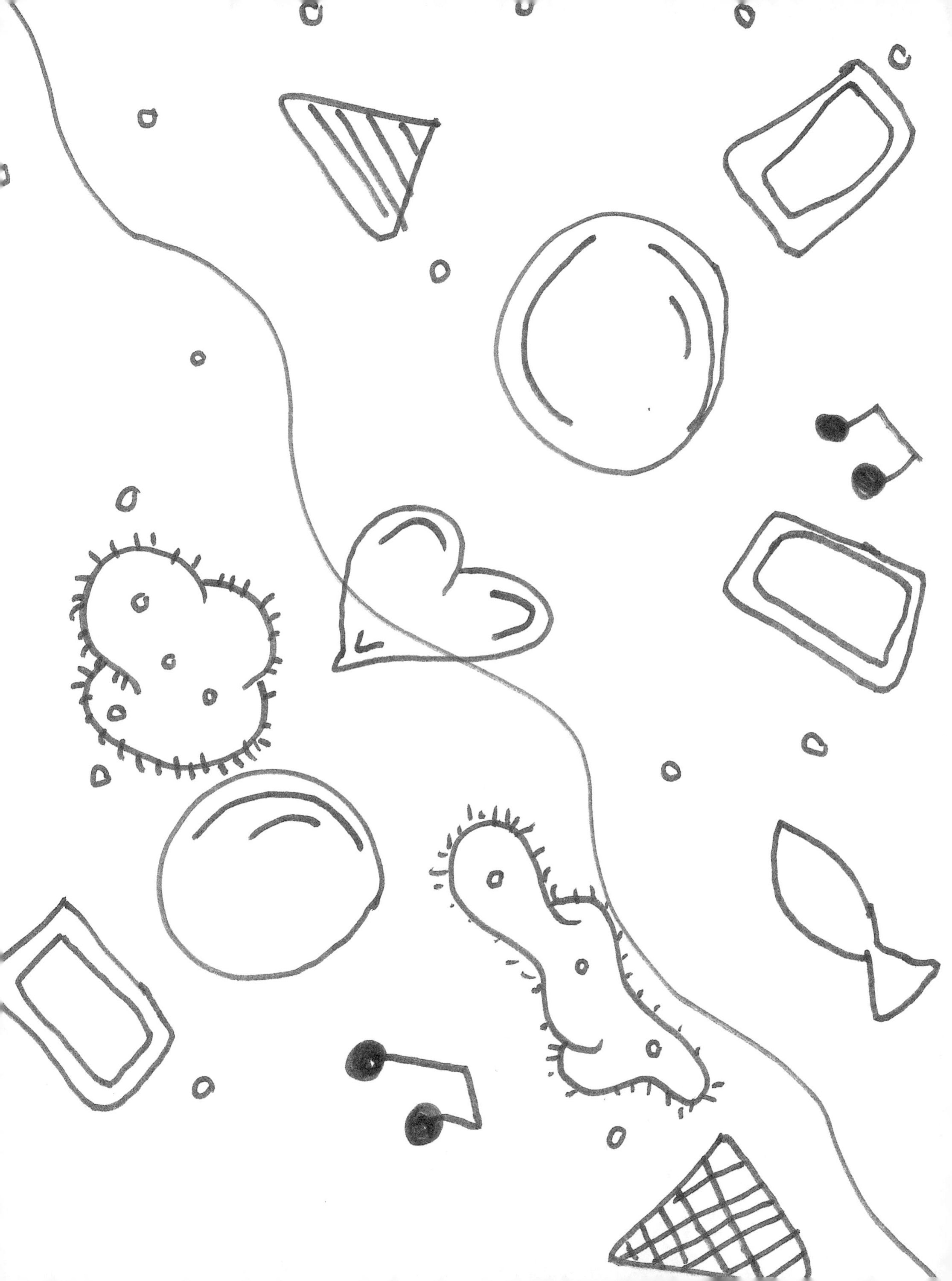

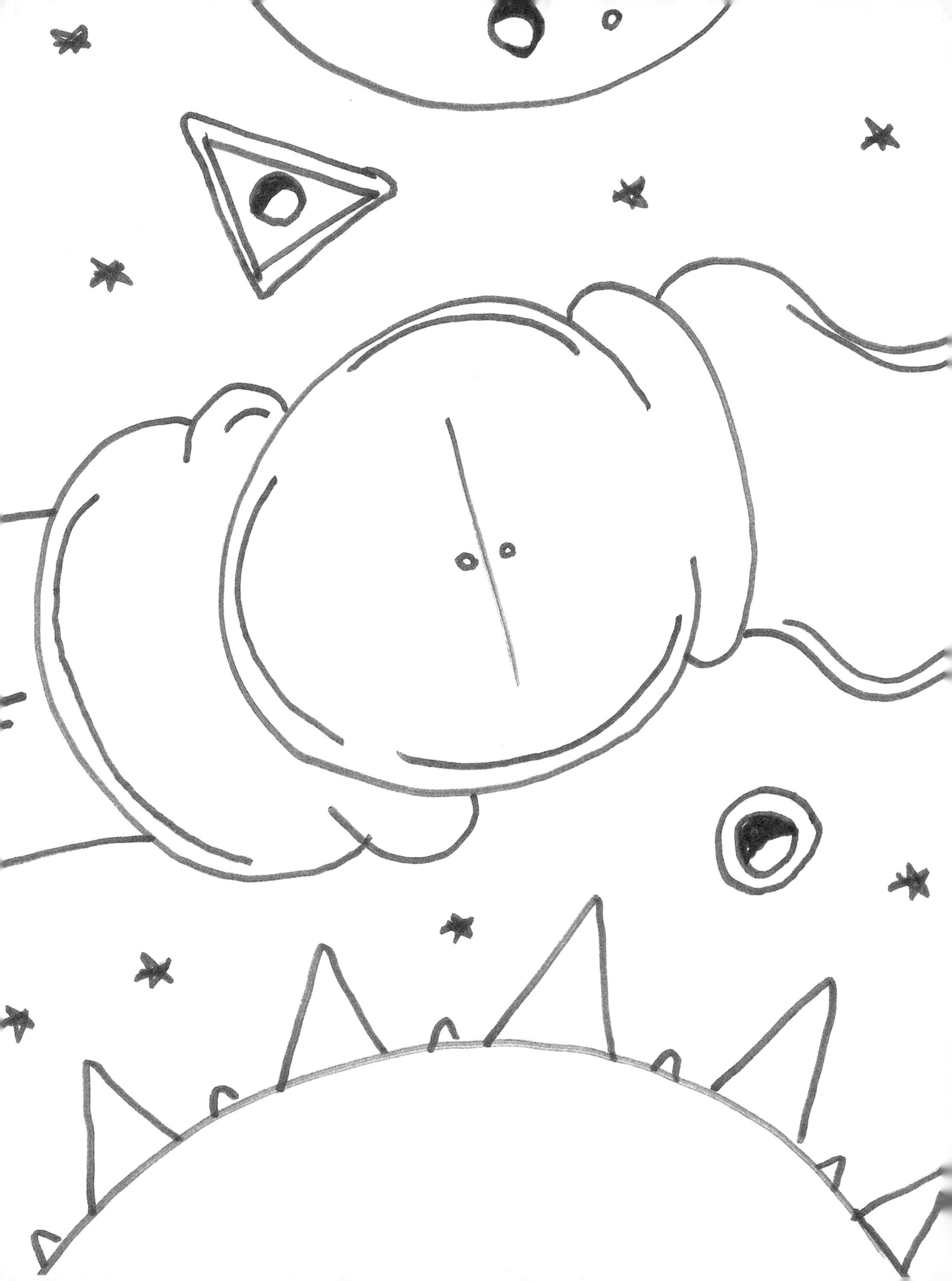

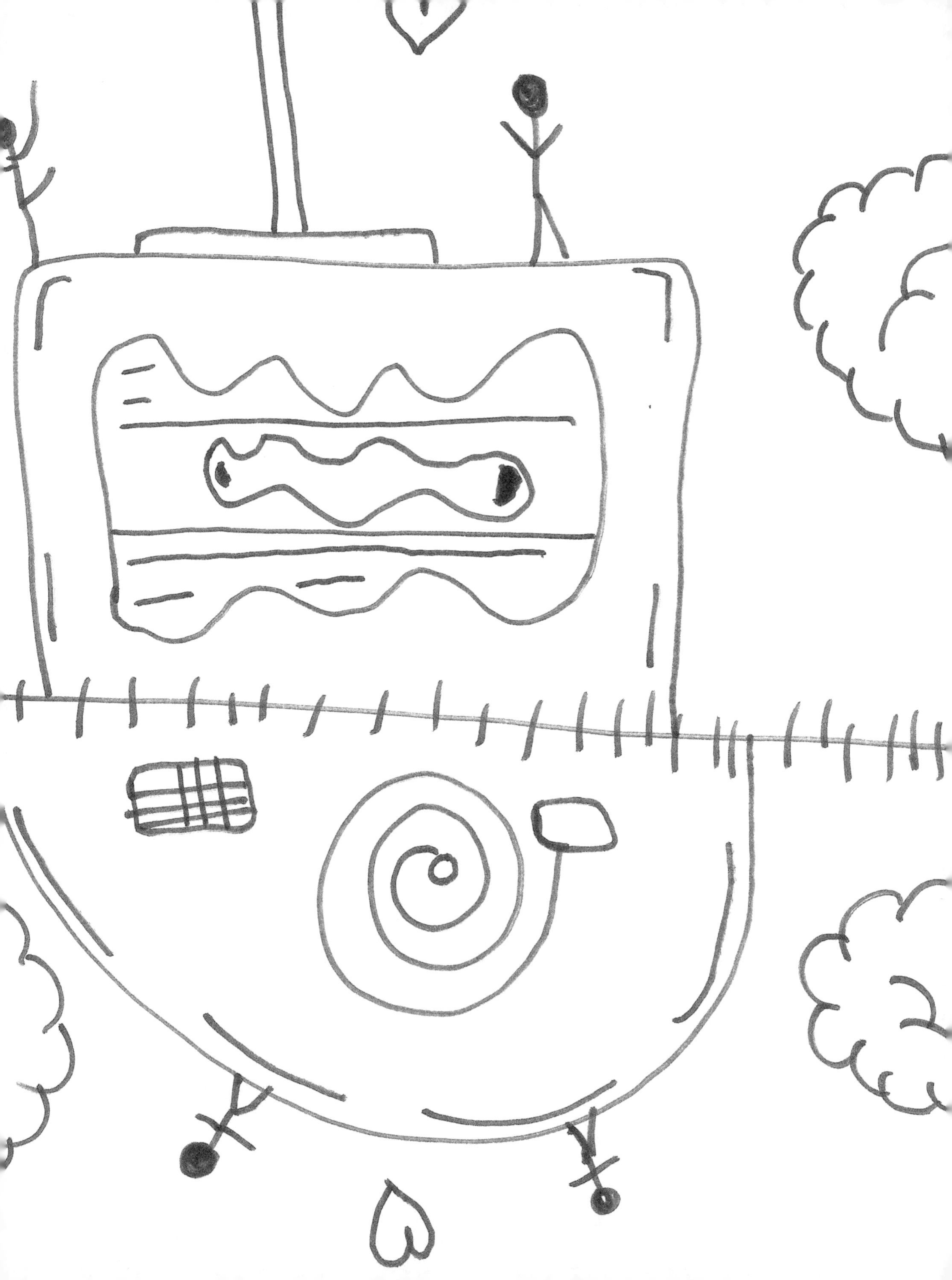

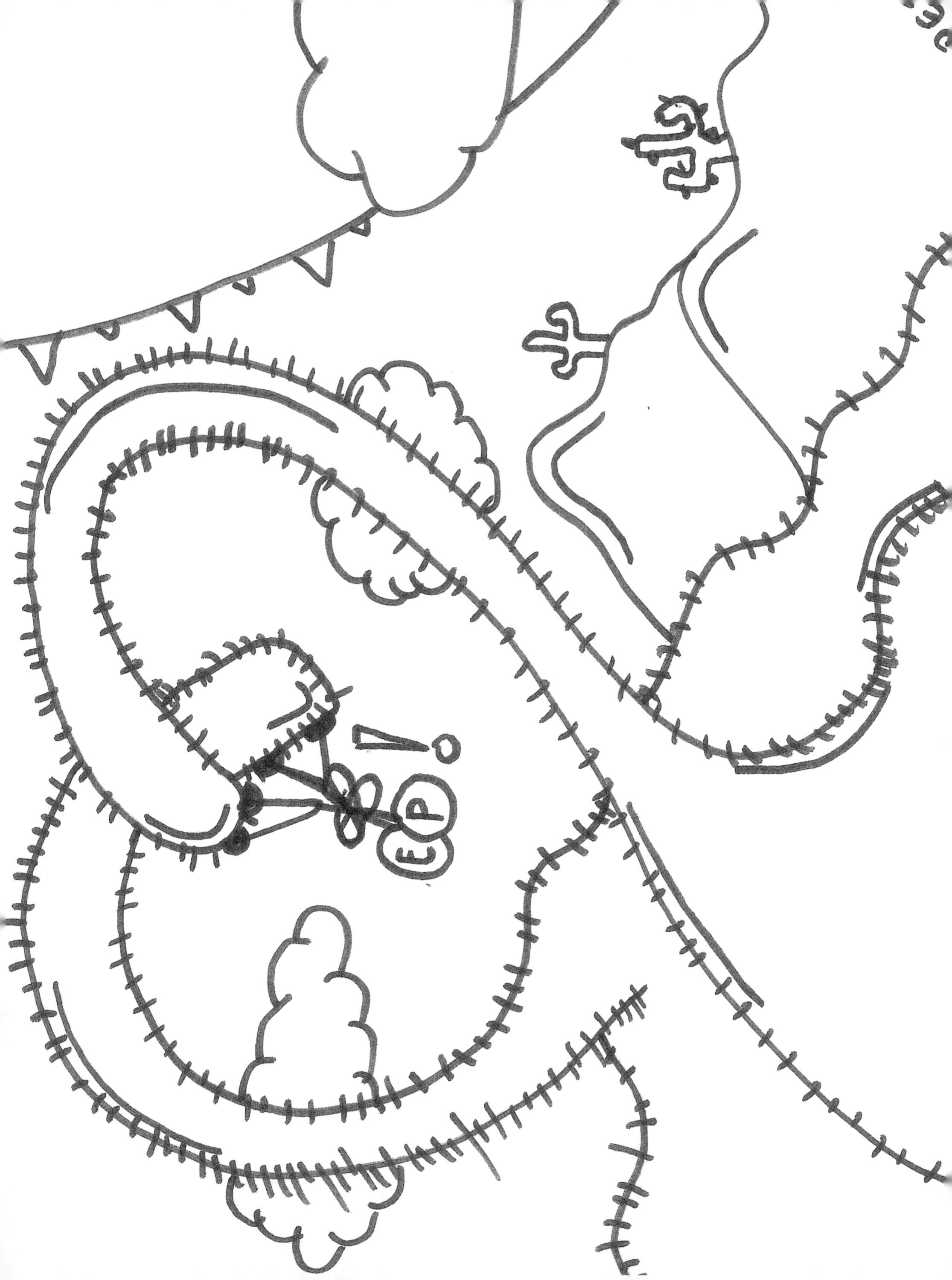

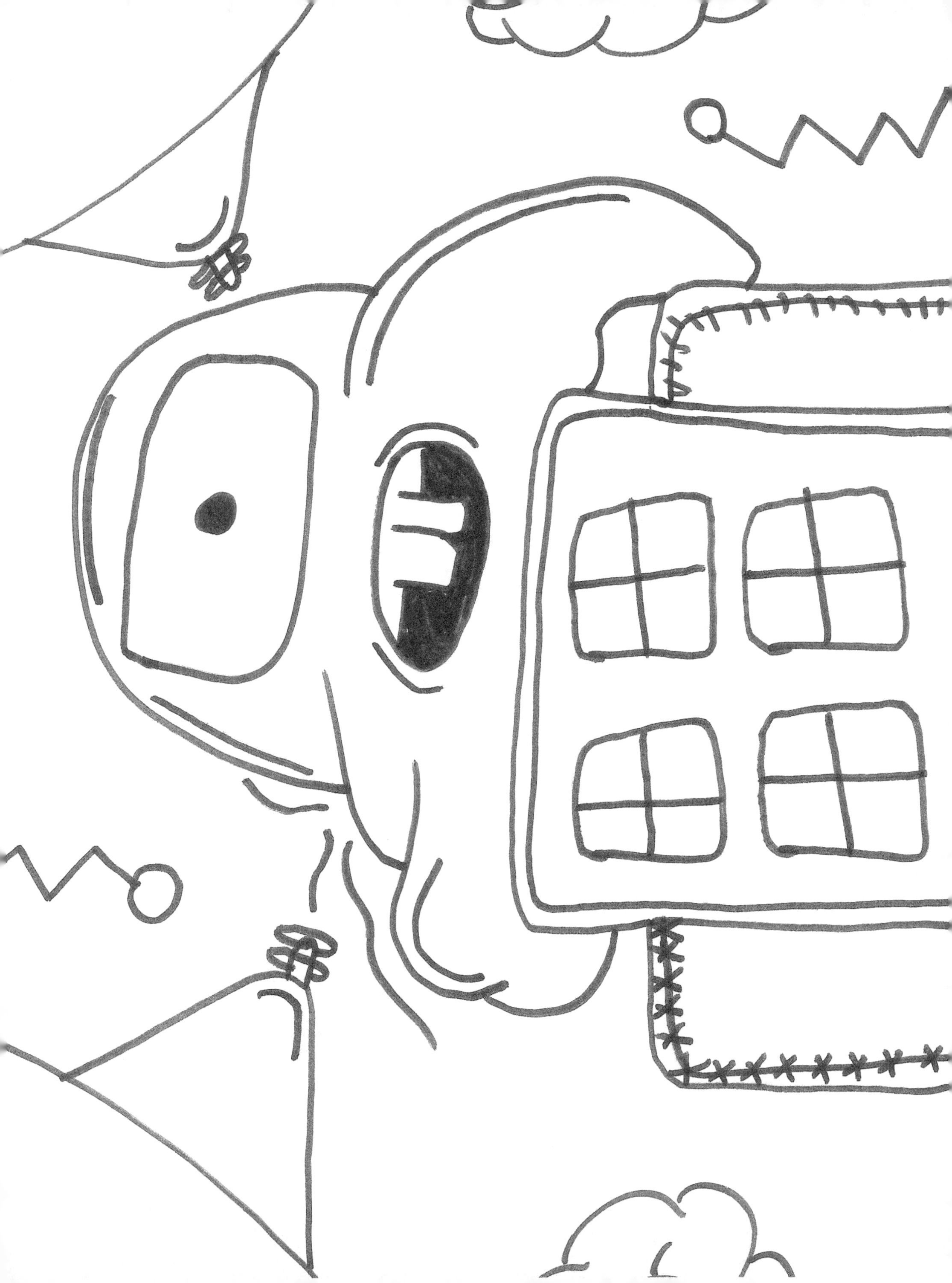

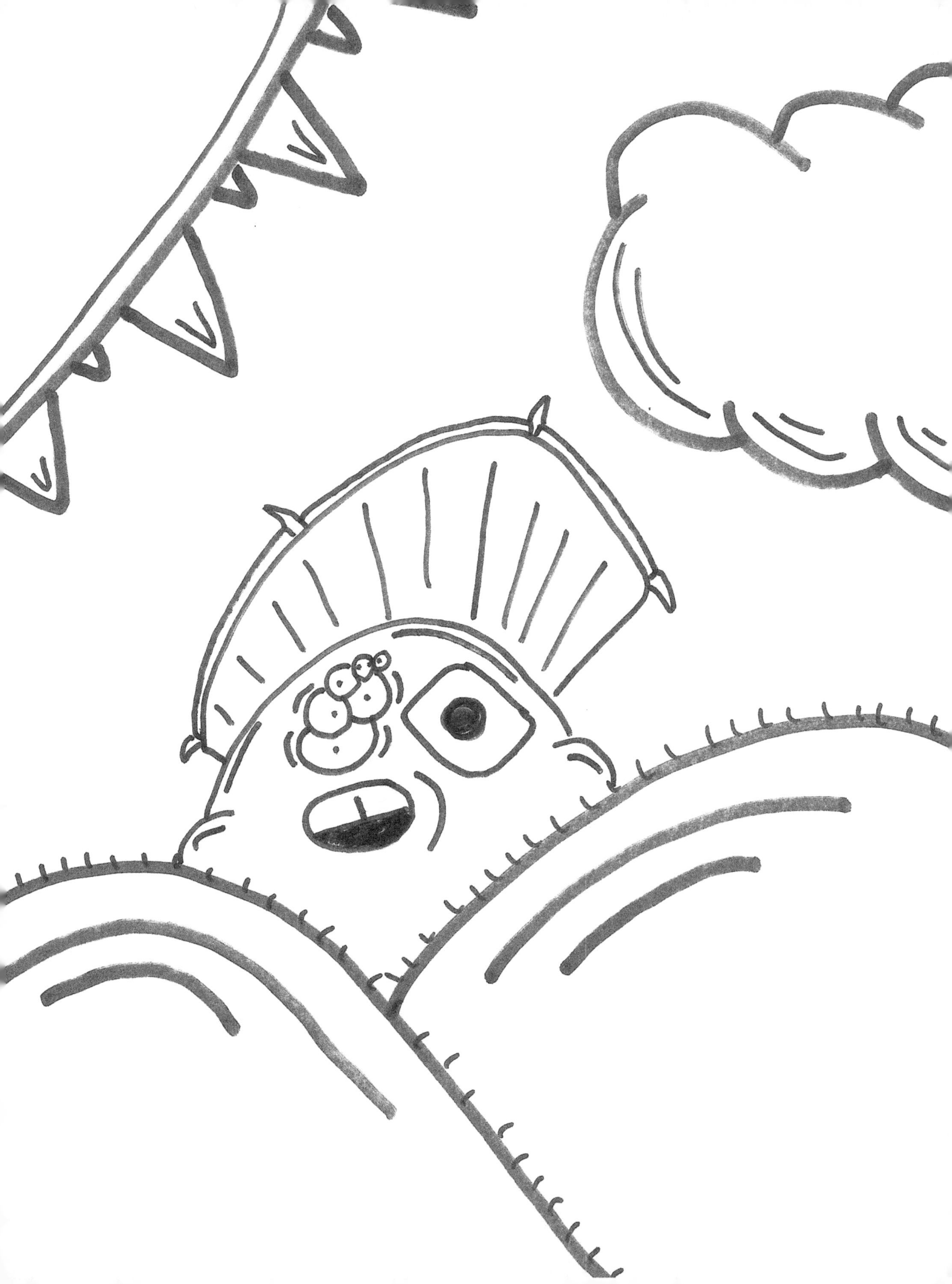

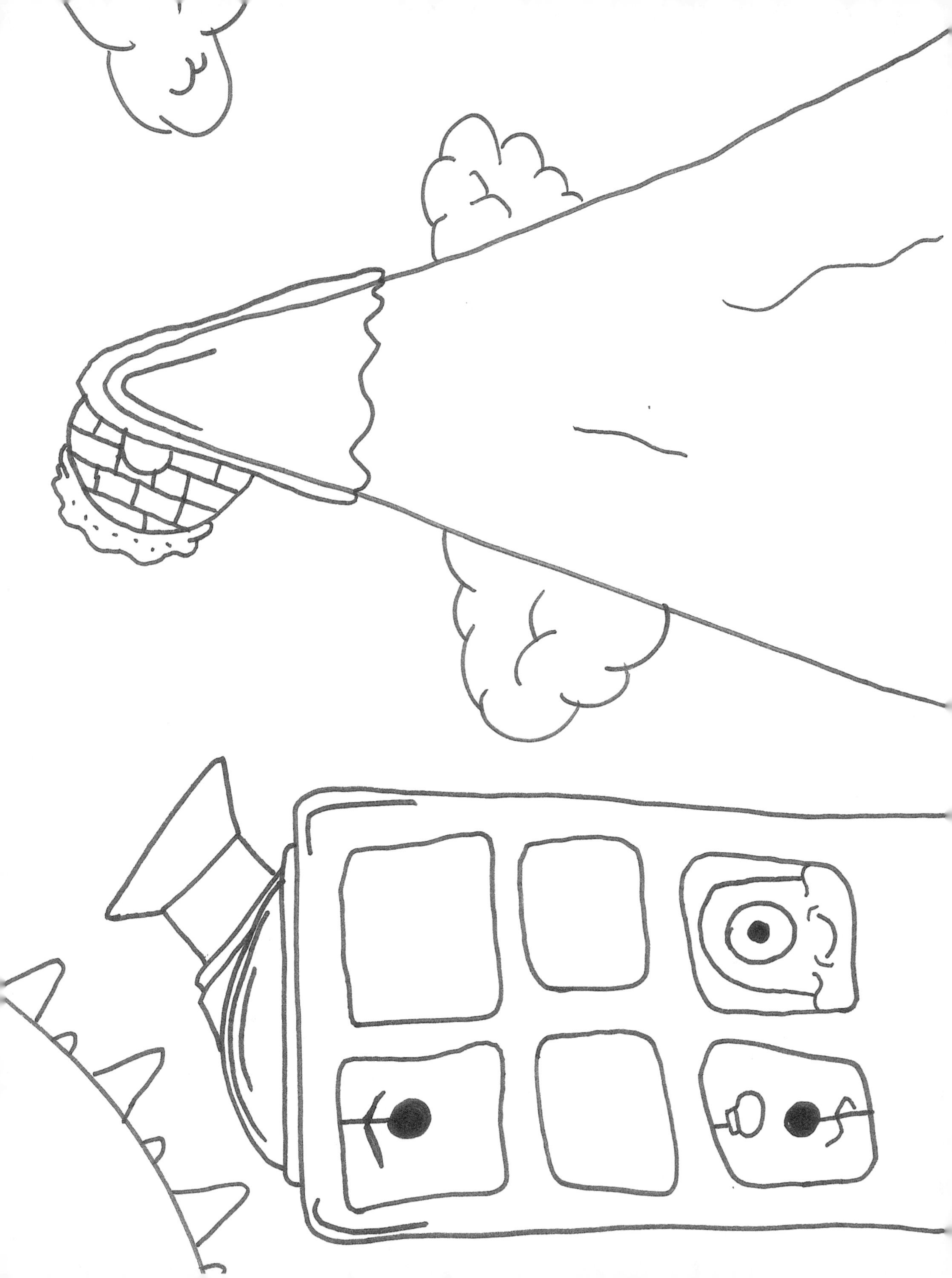

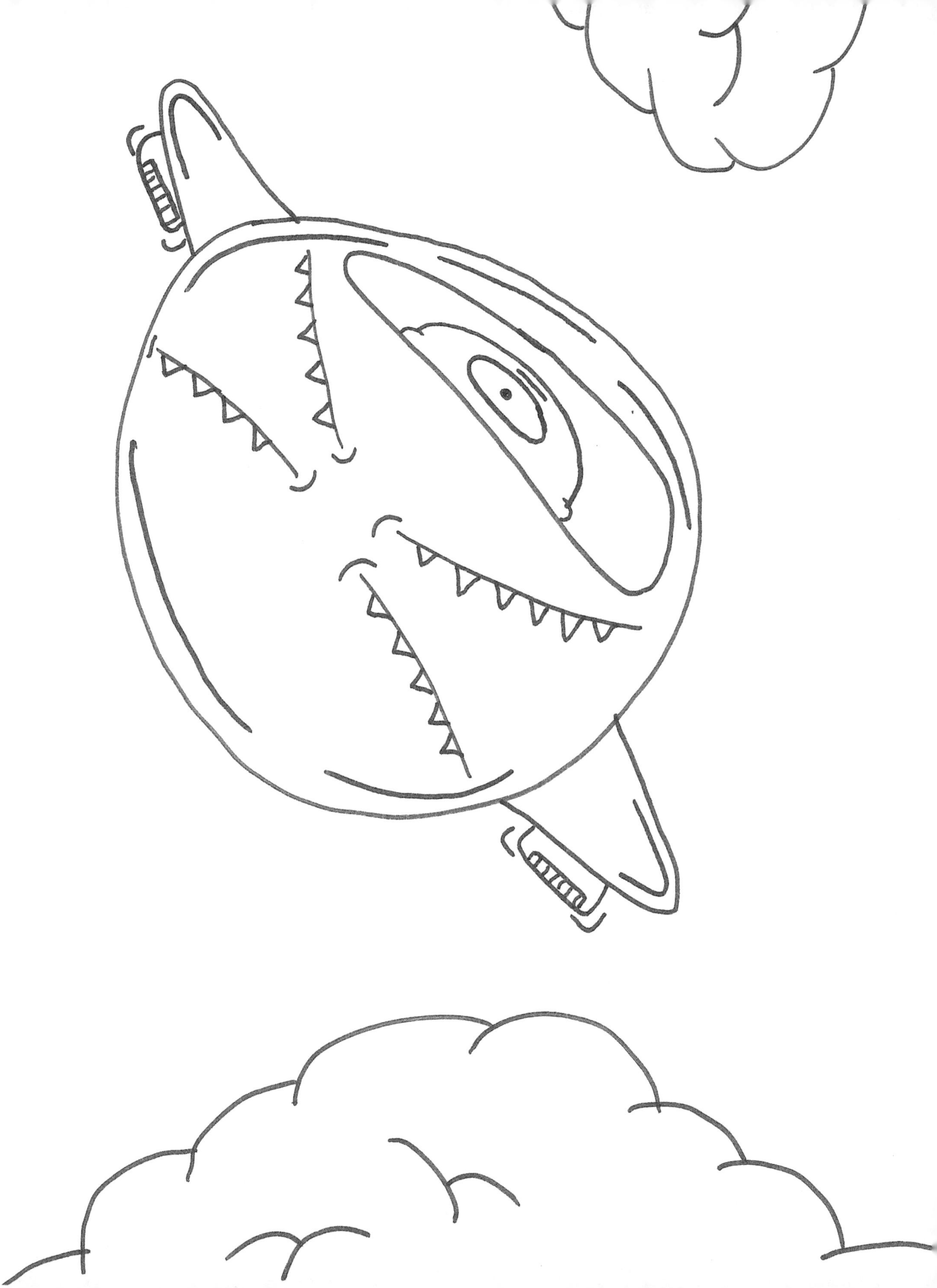

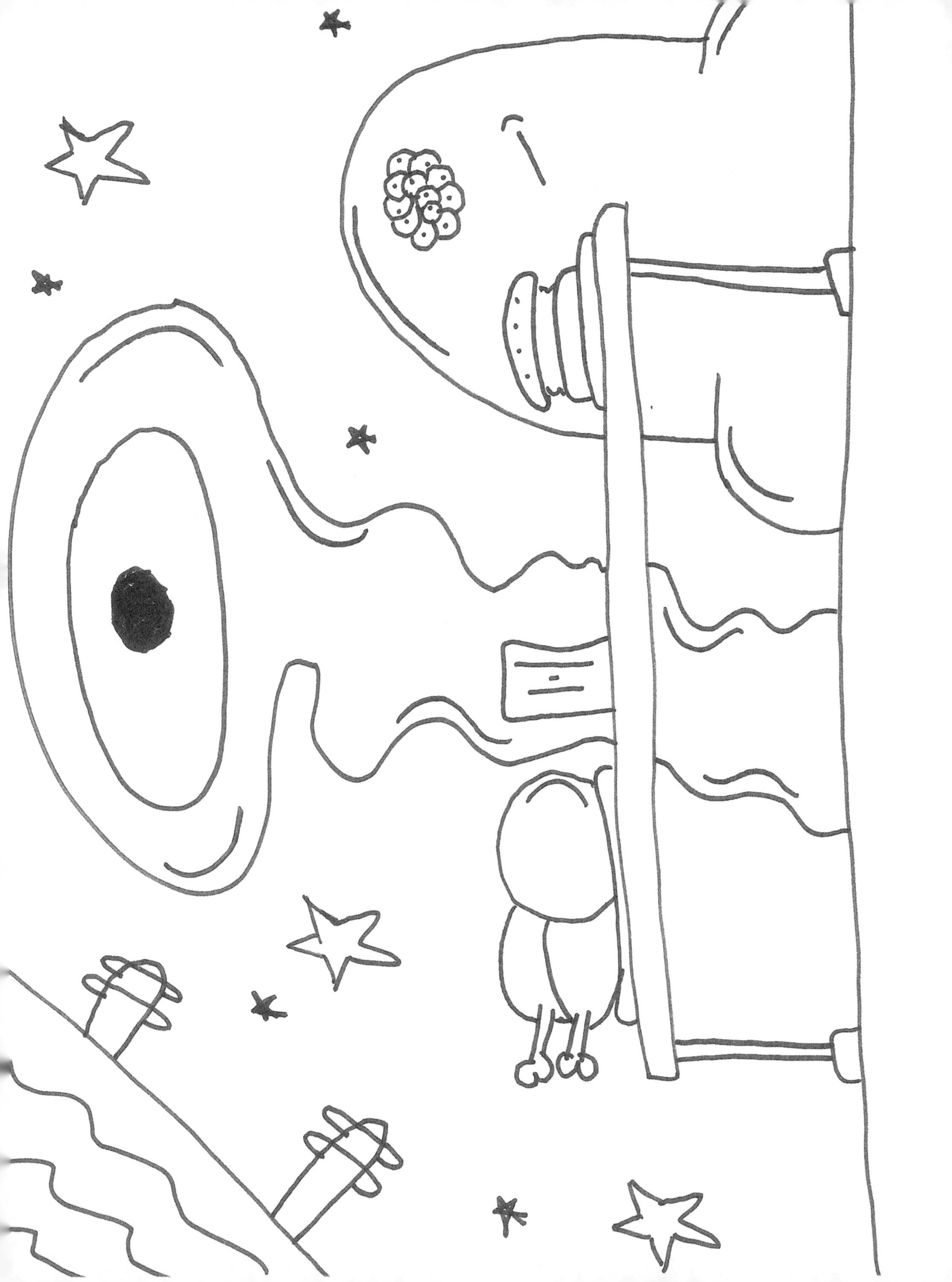

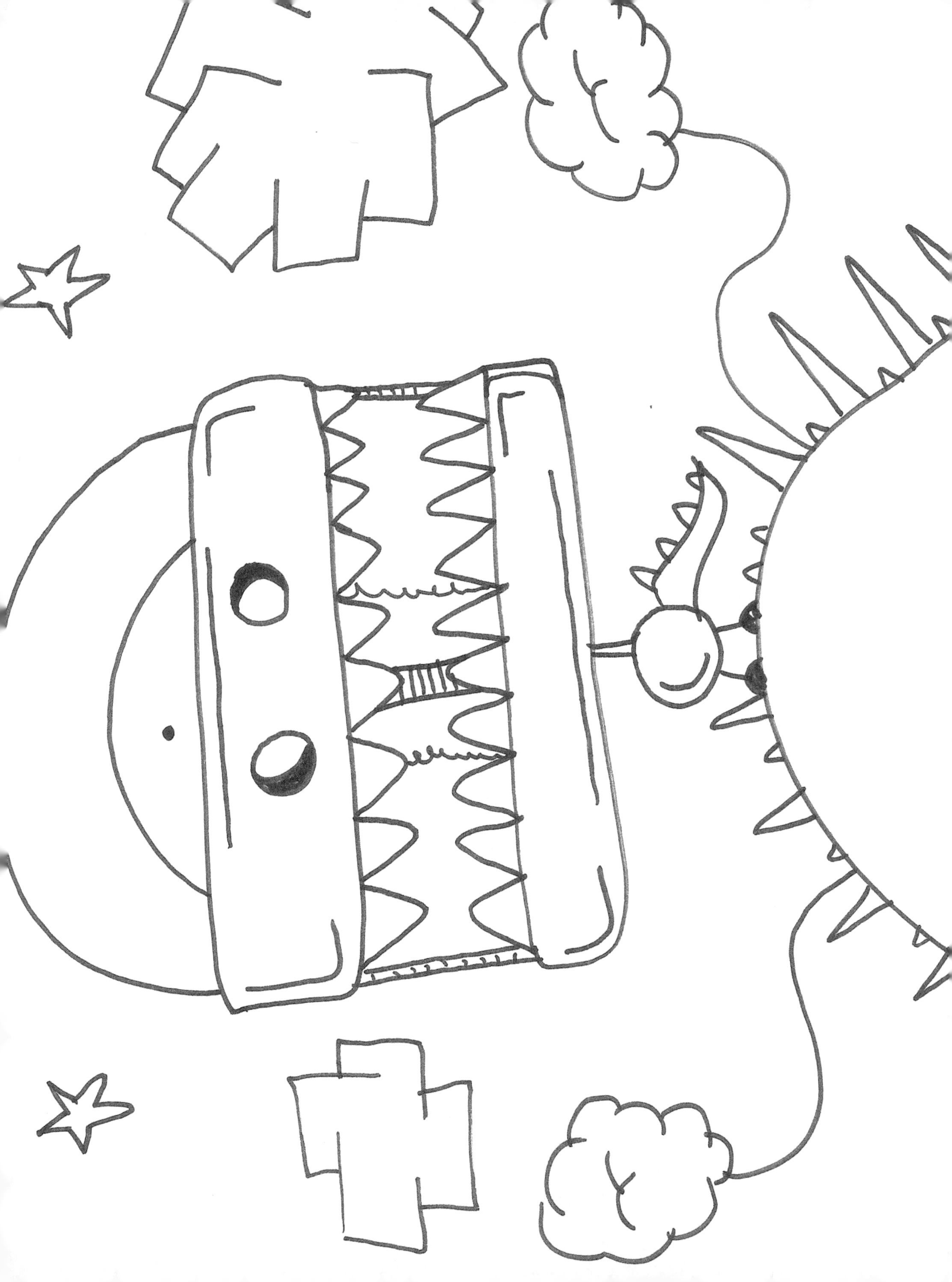

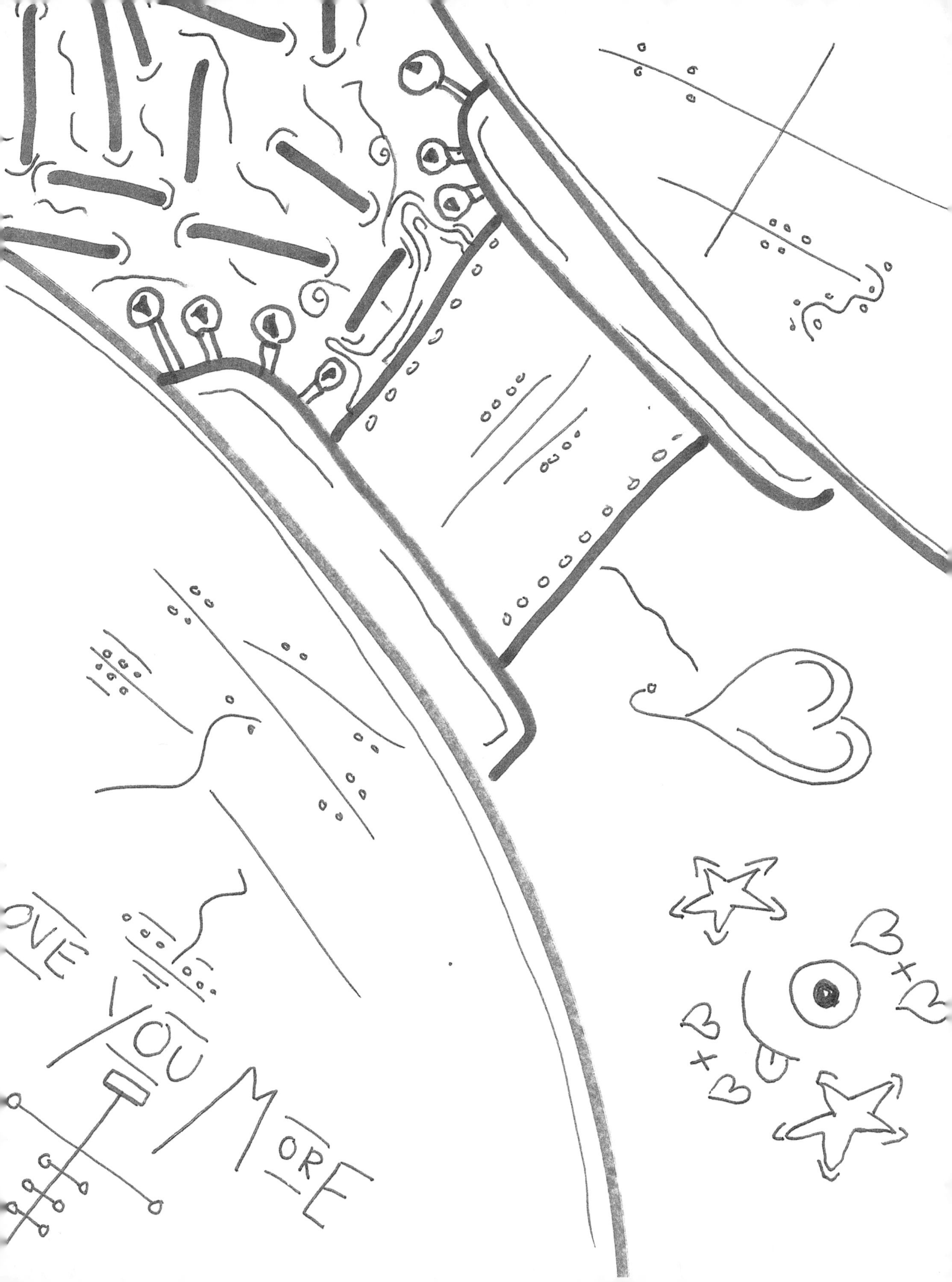
OVE
YOU
MORE
ORE

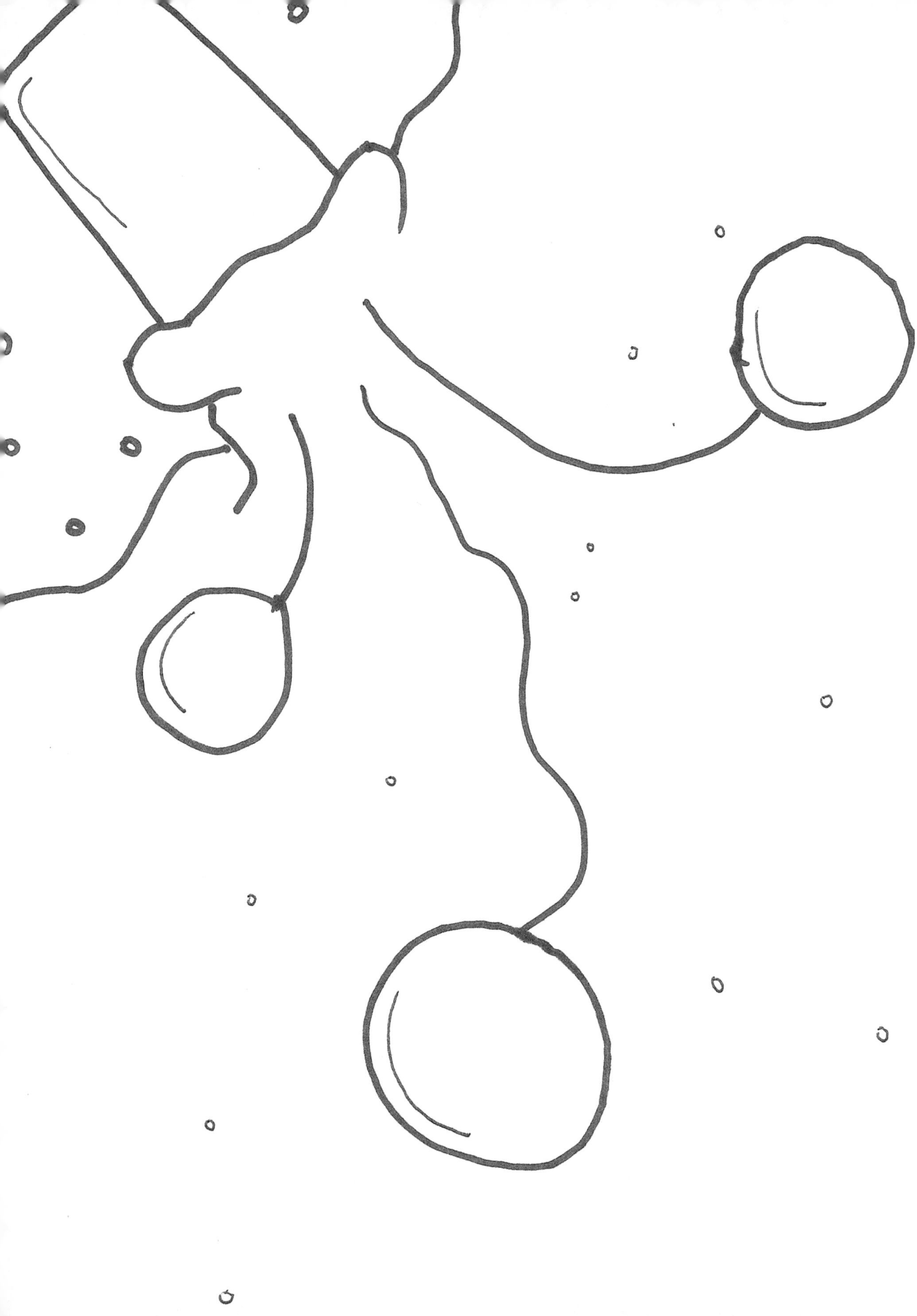

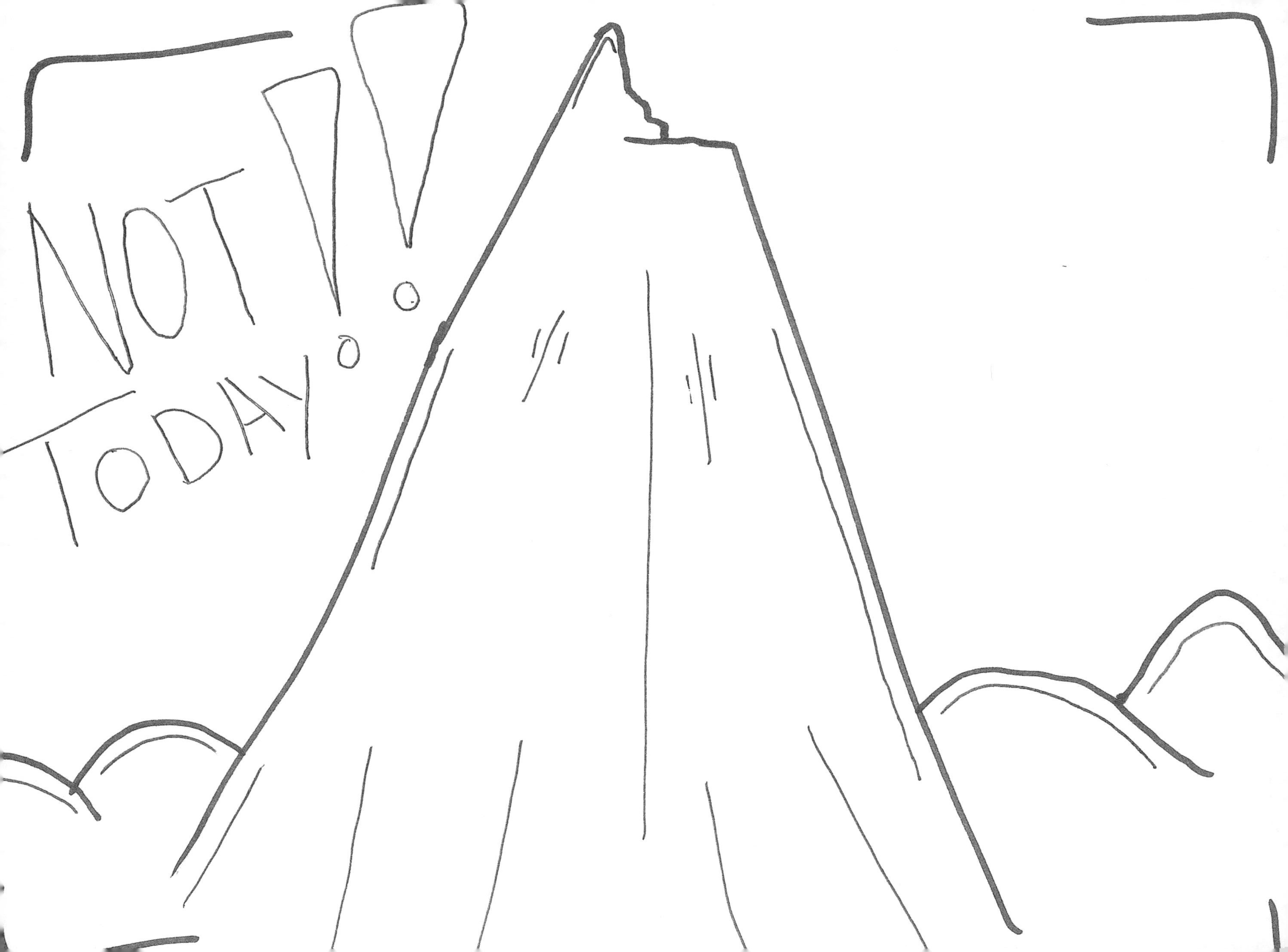
NOT TODAY!!

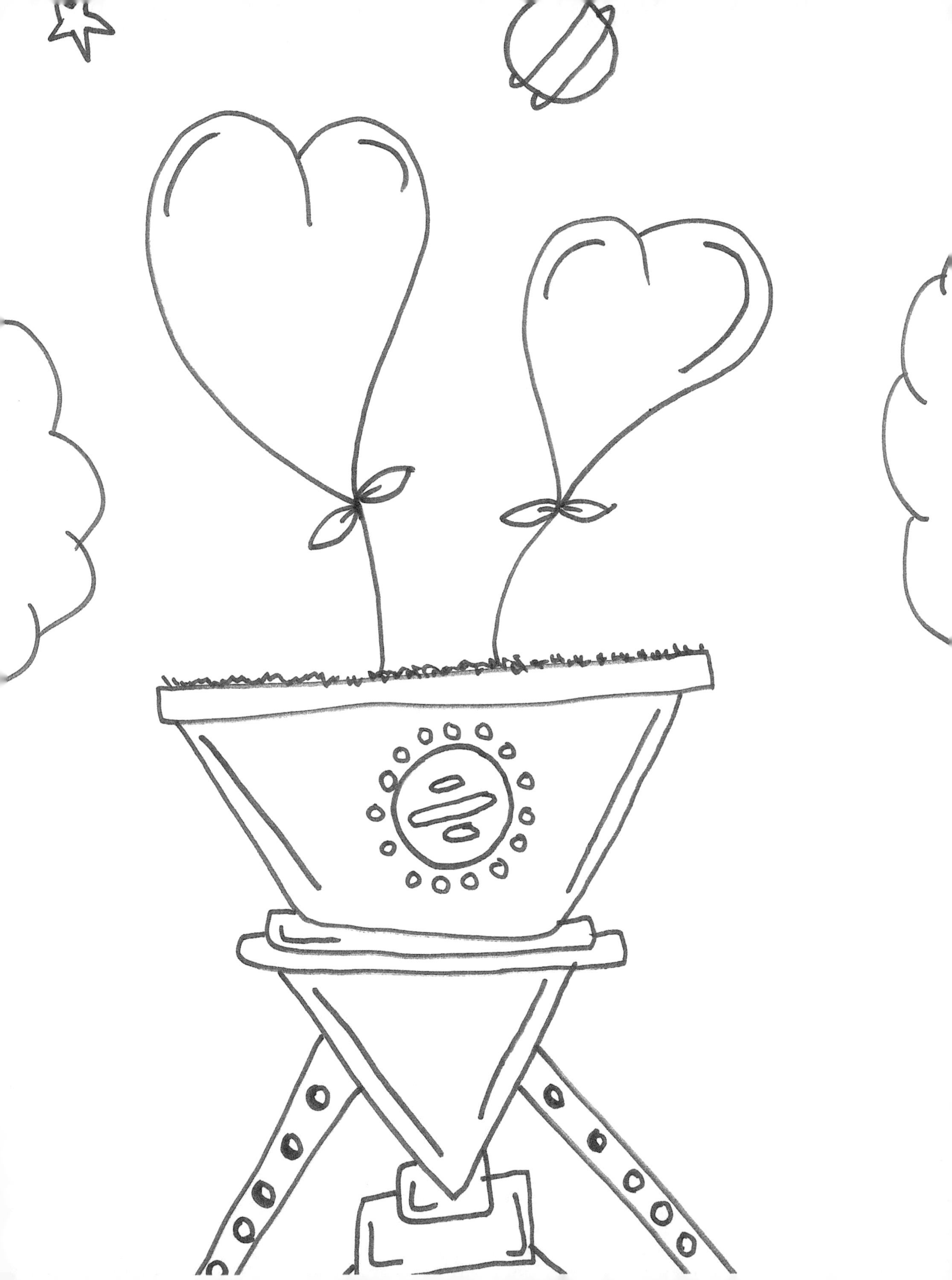

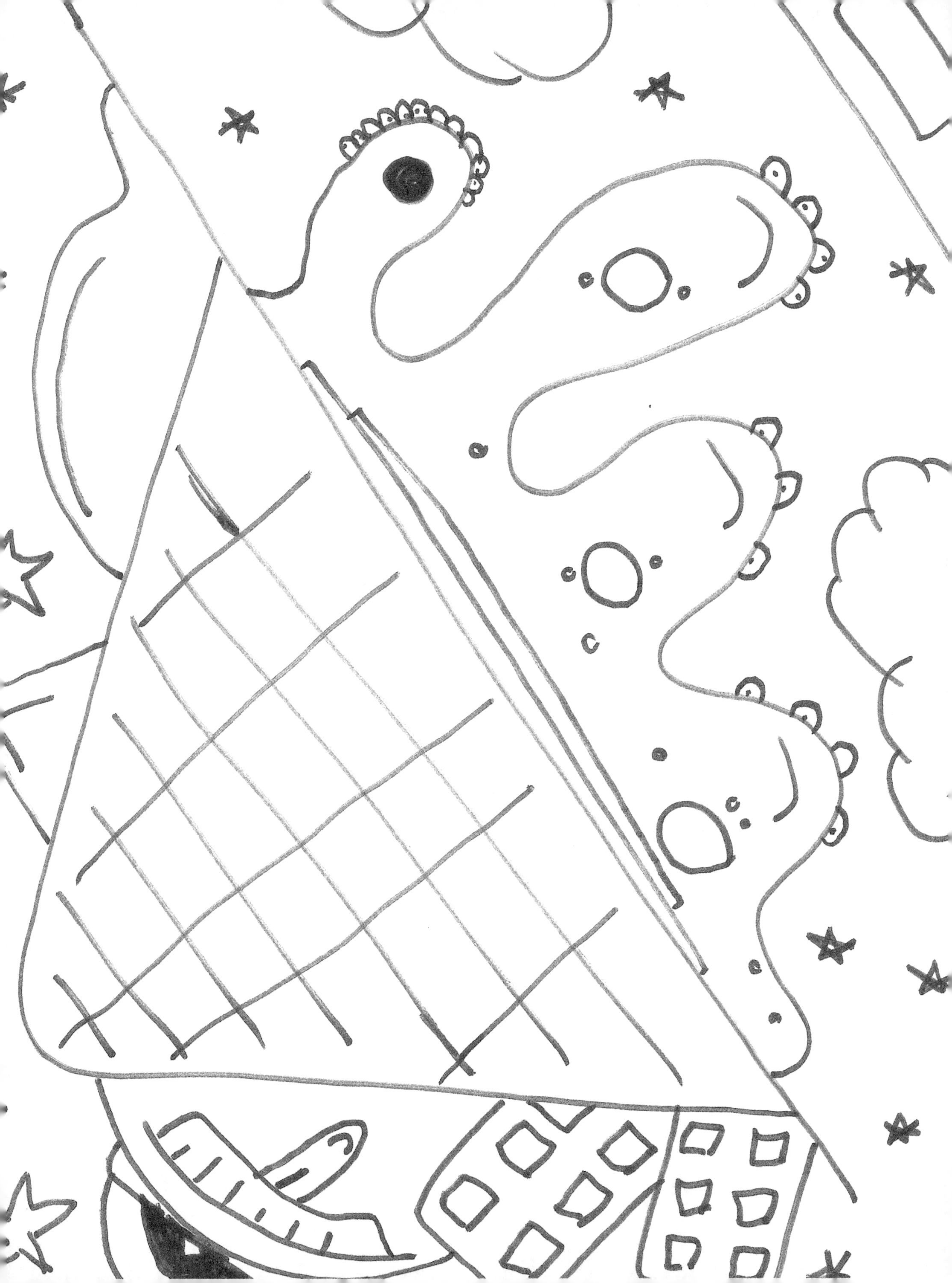

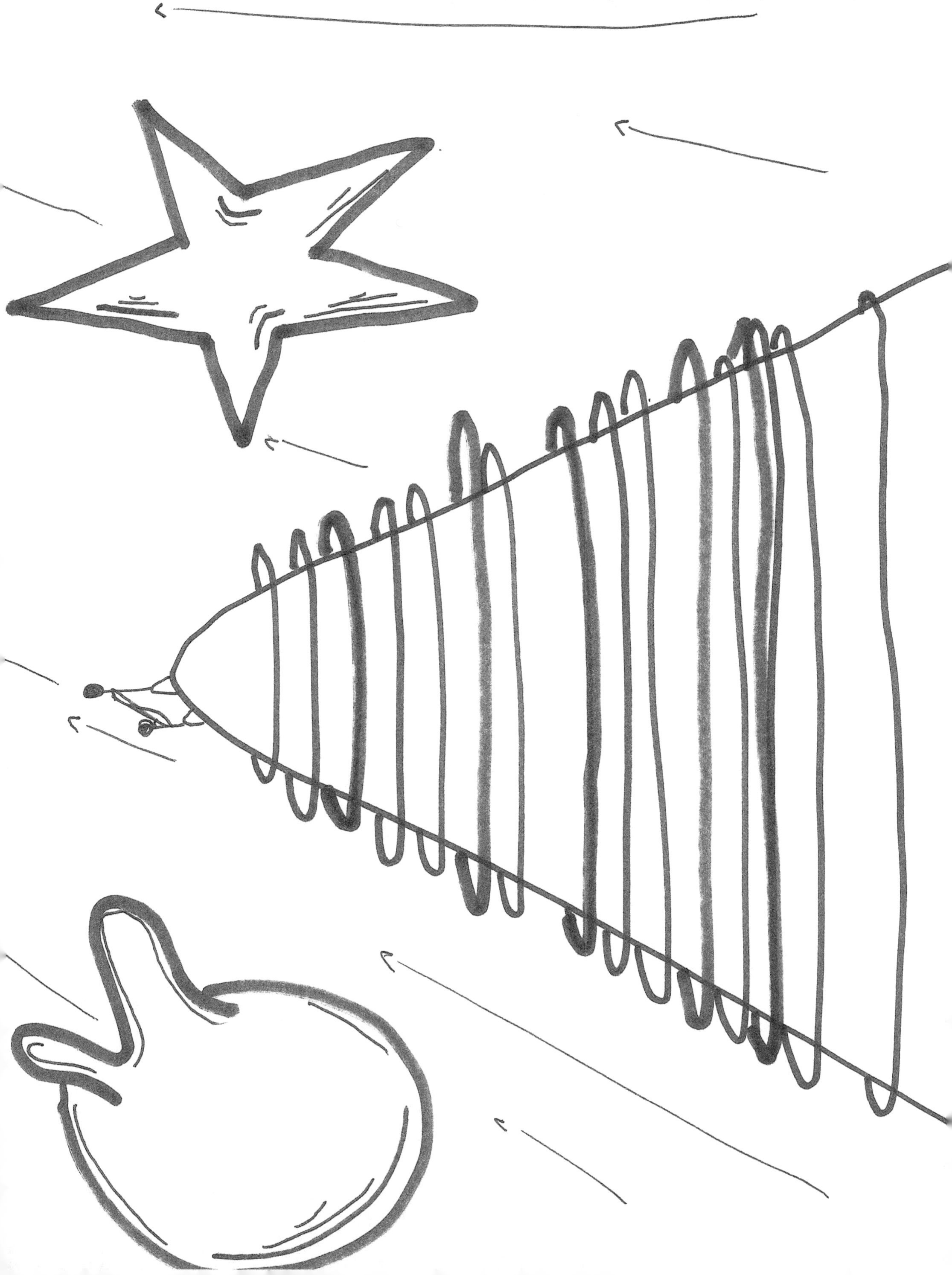

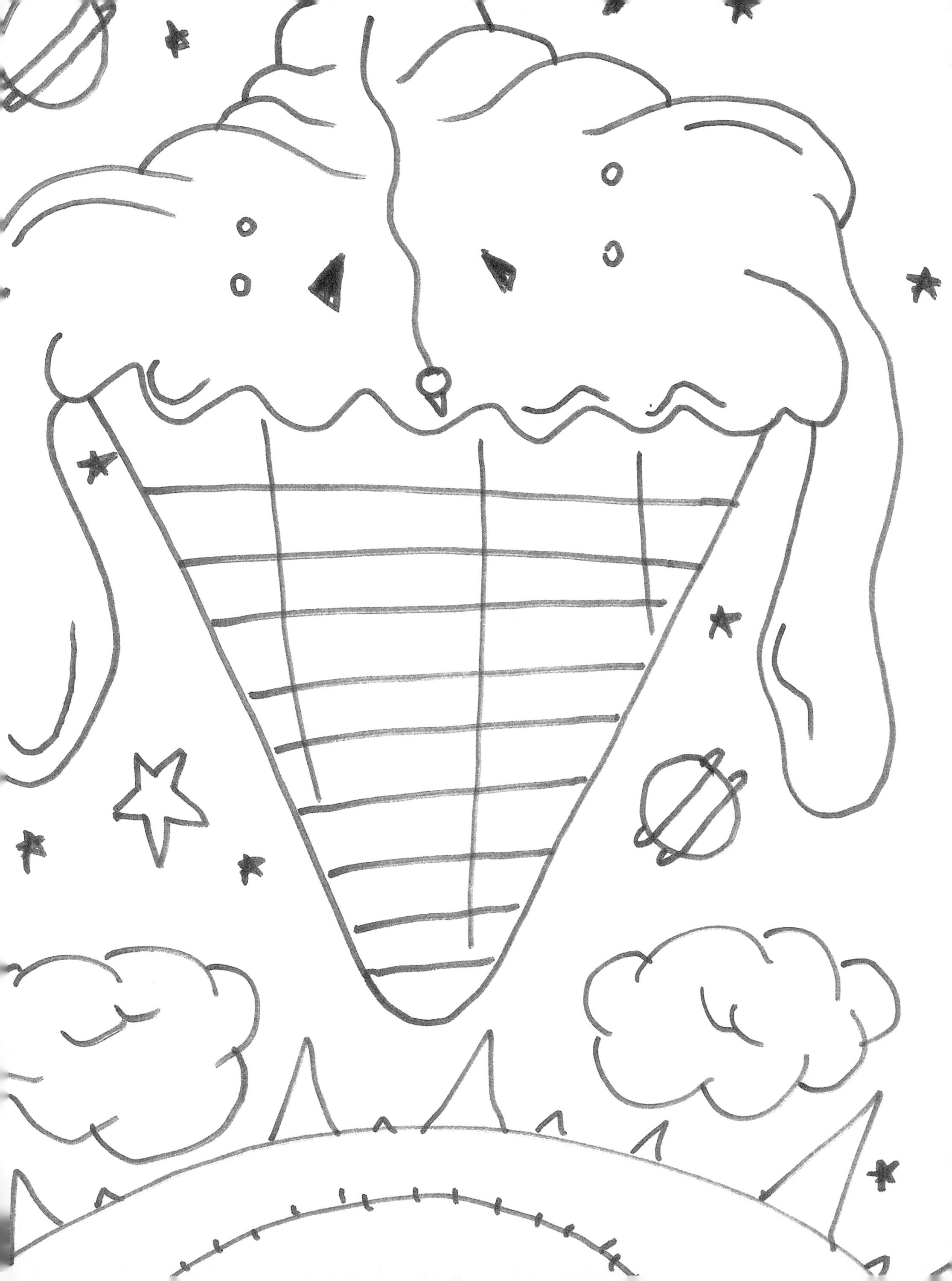

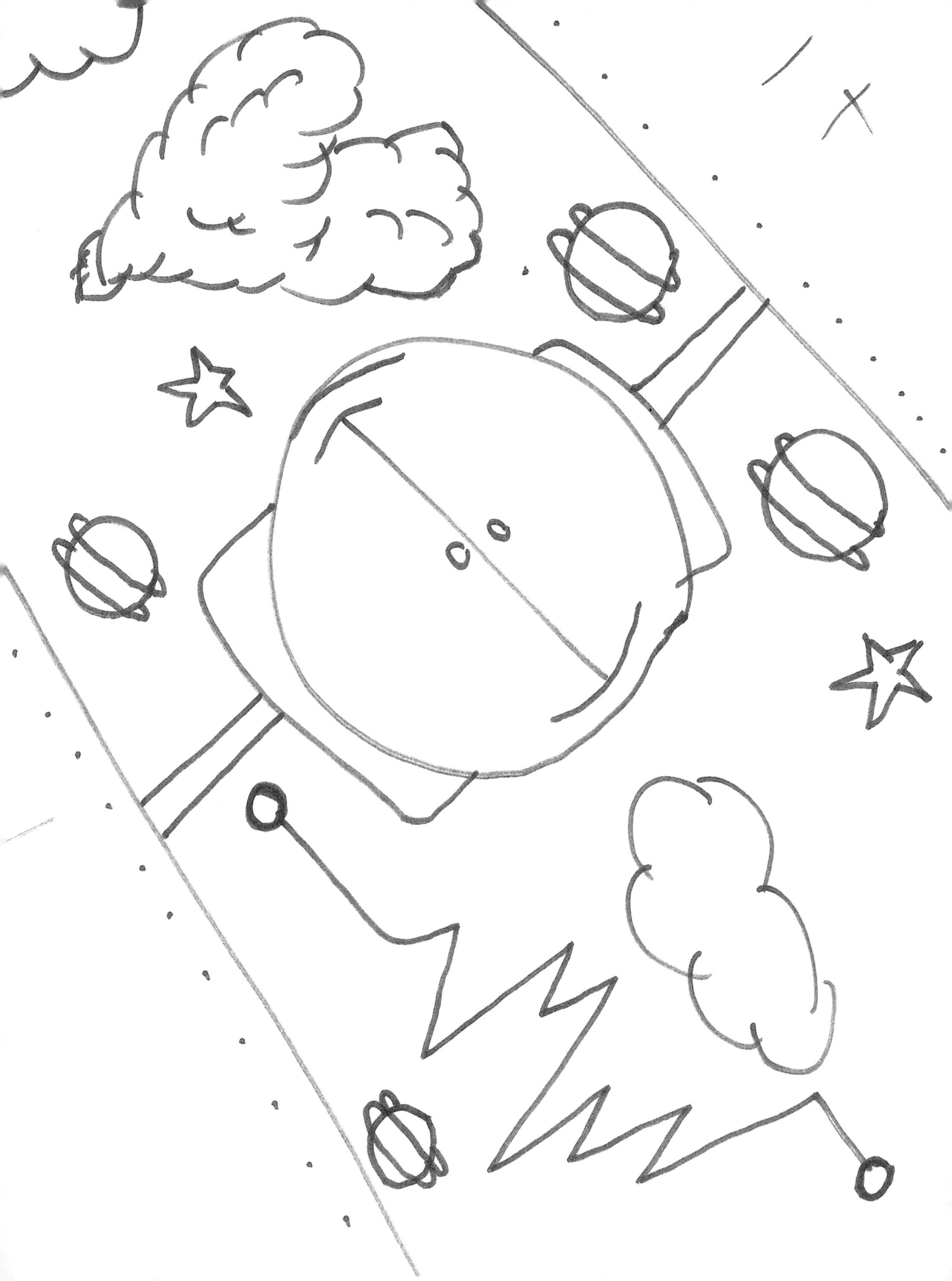

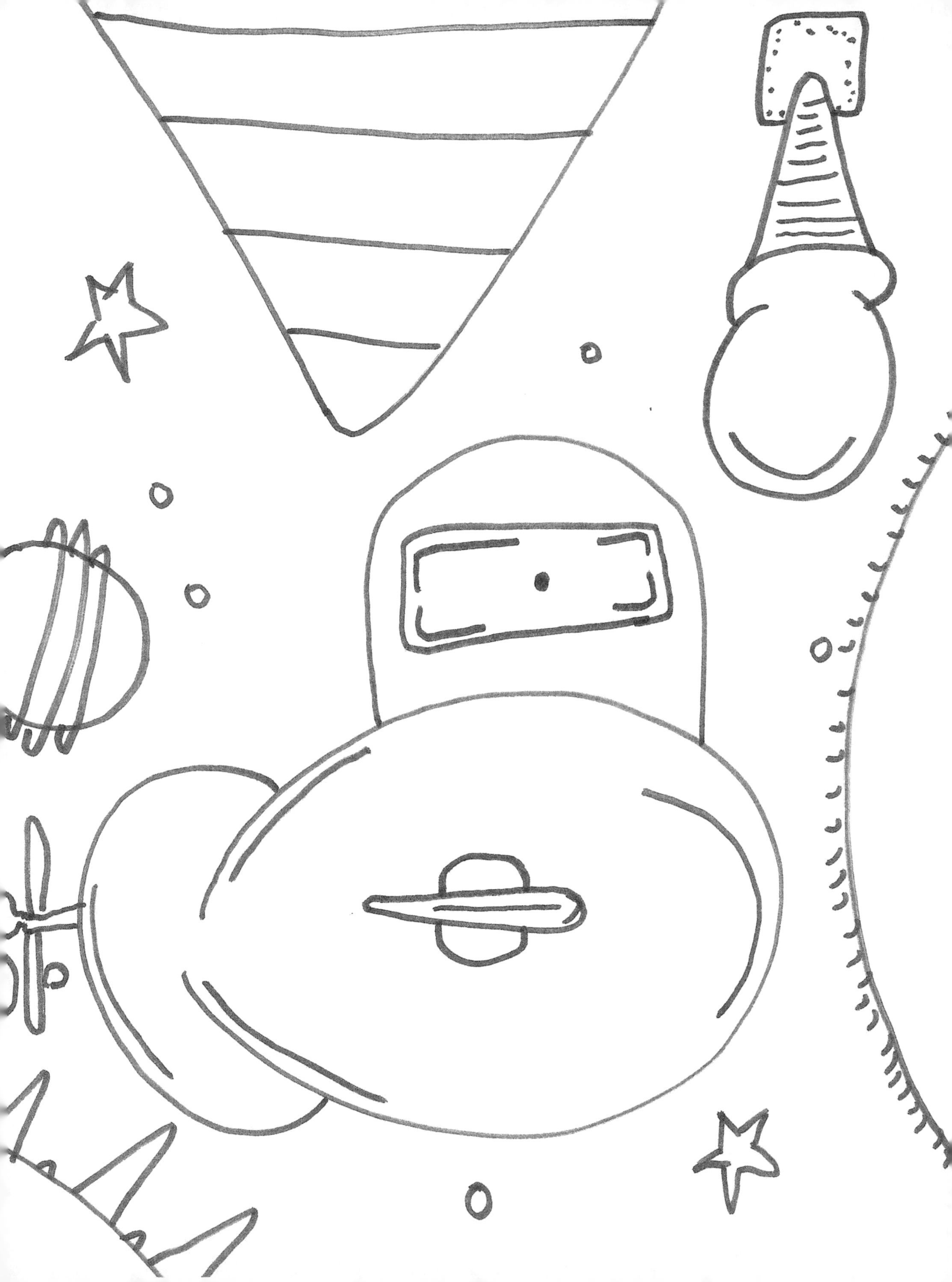

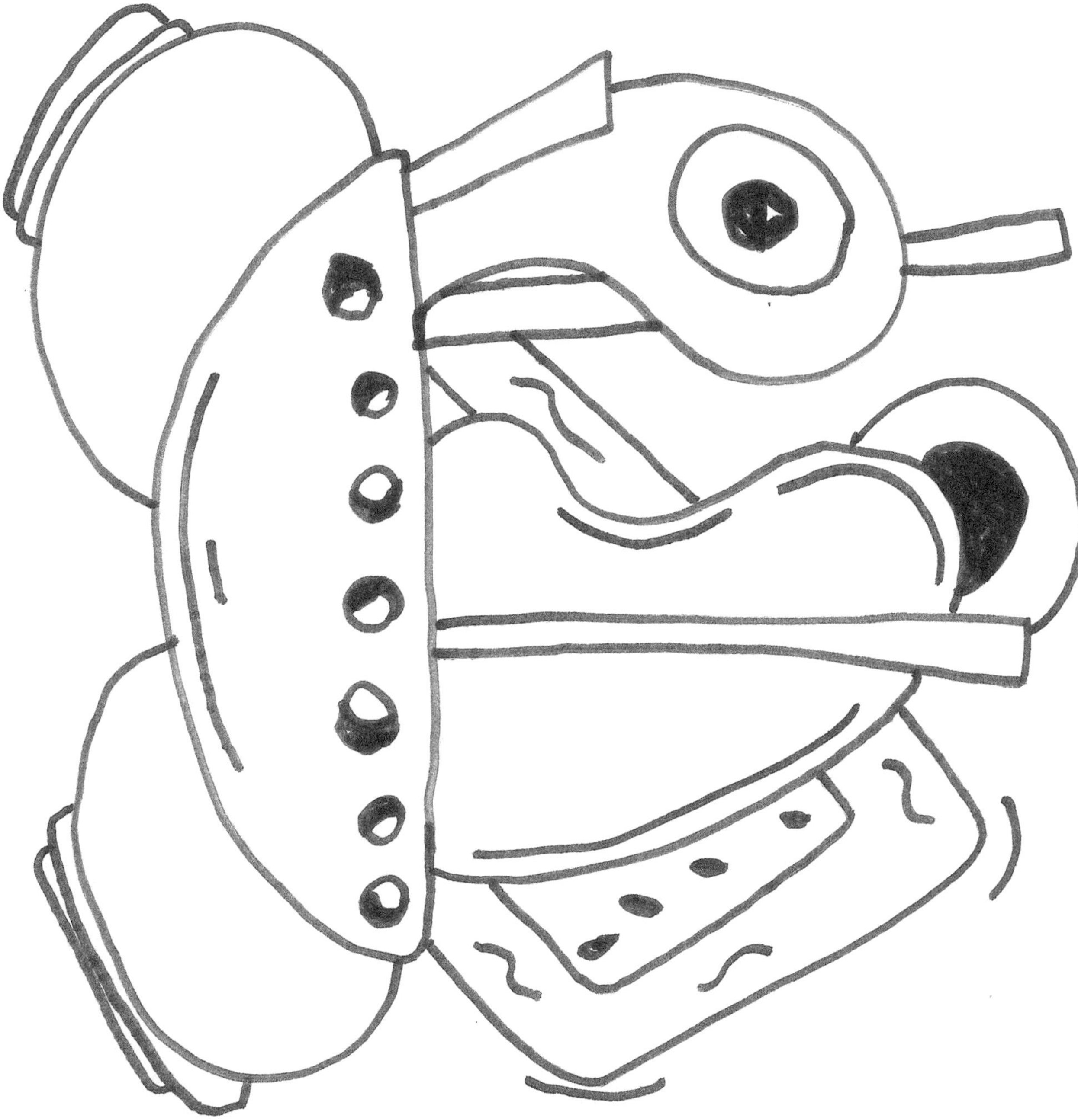

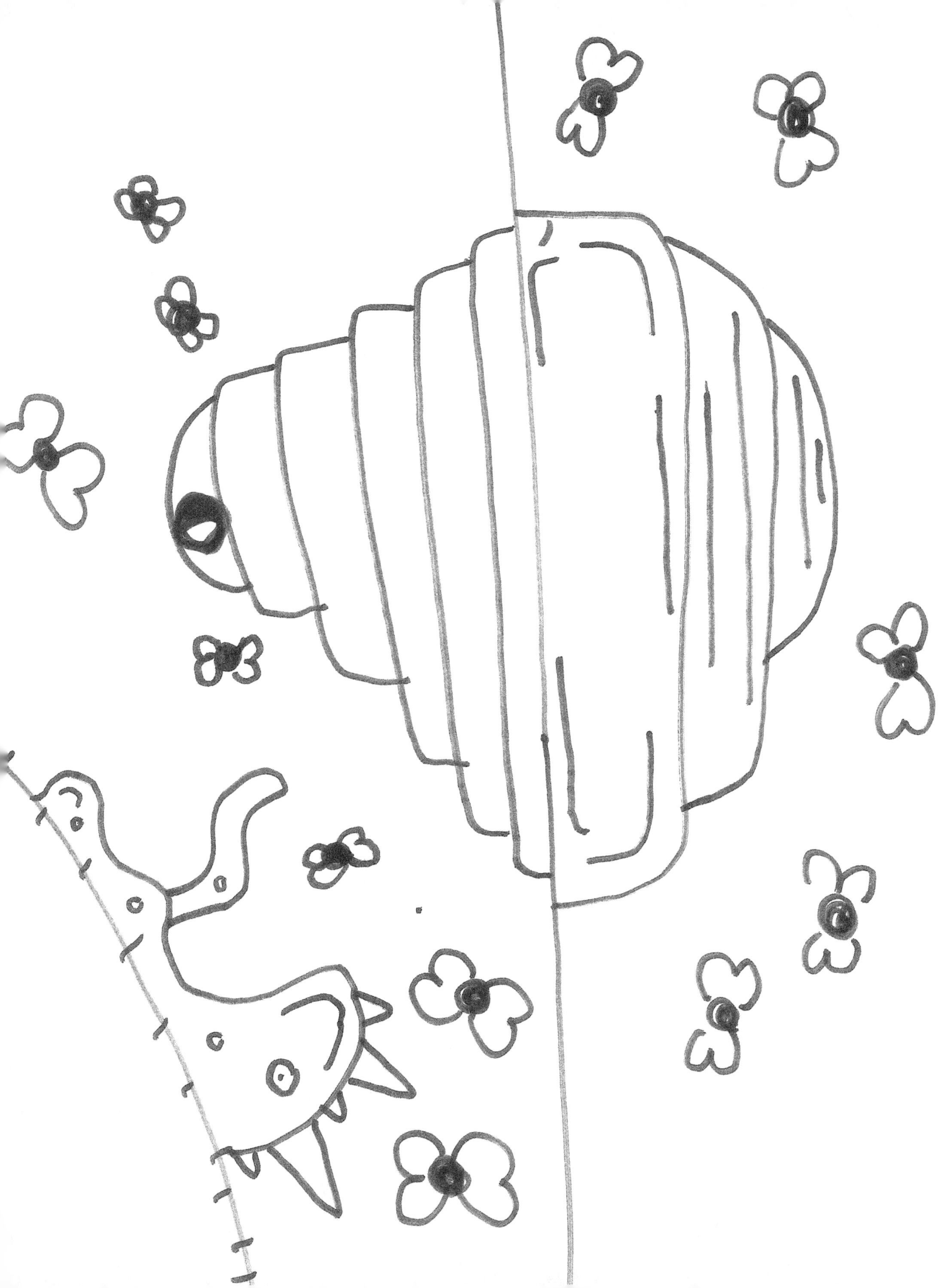

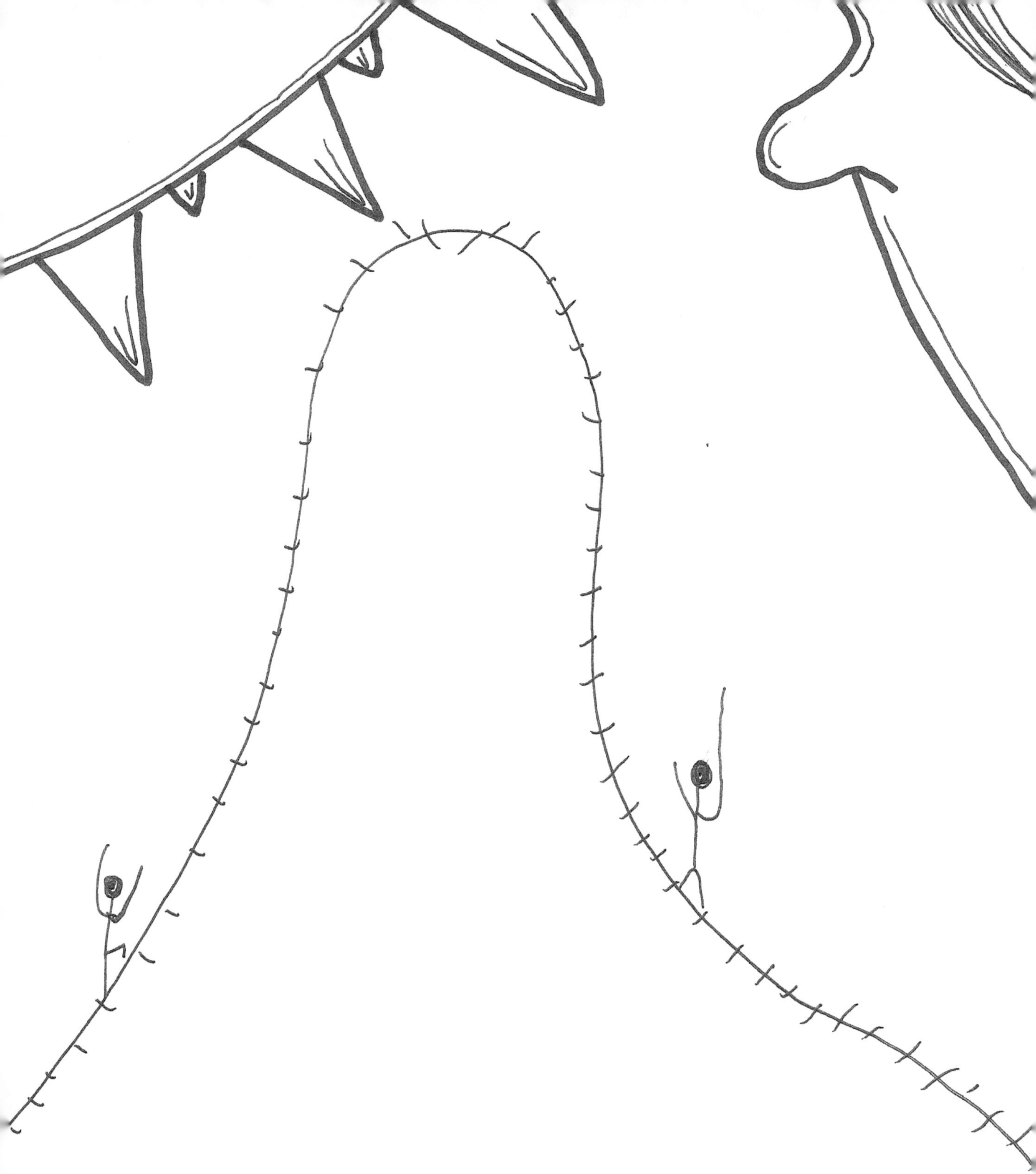

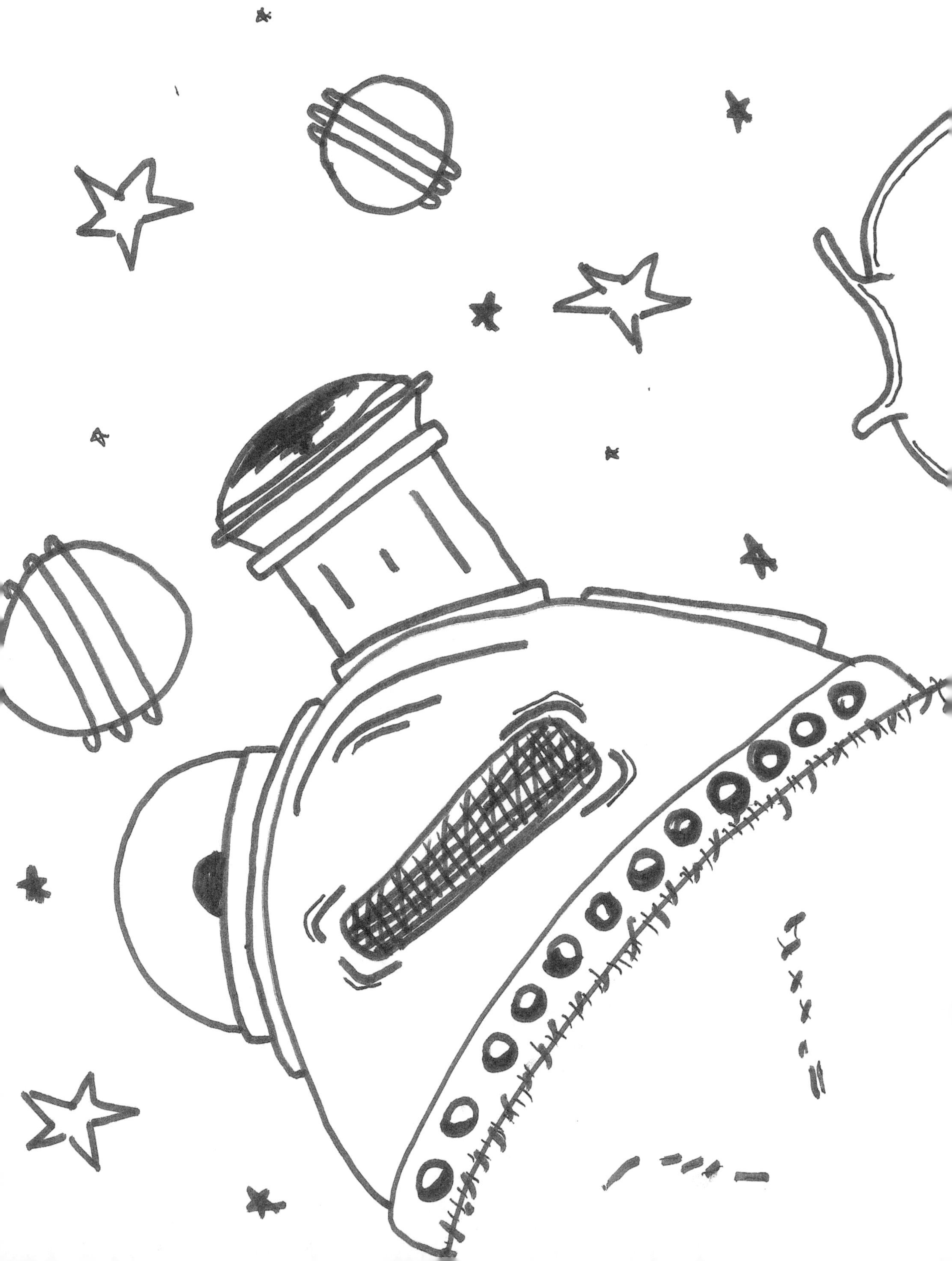

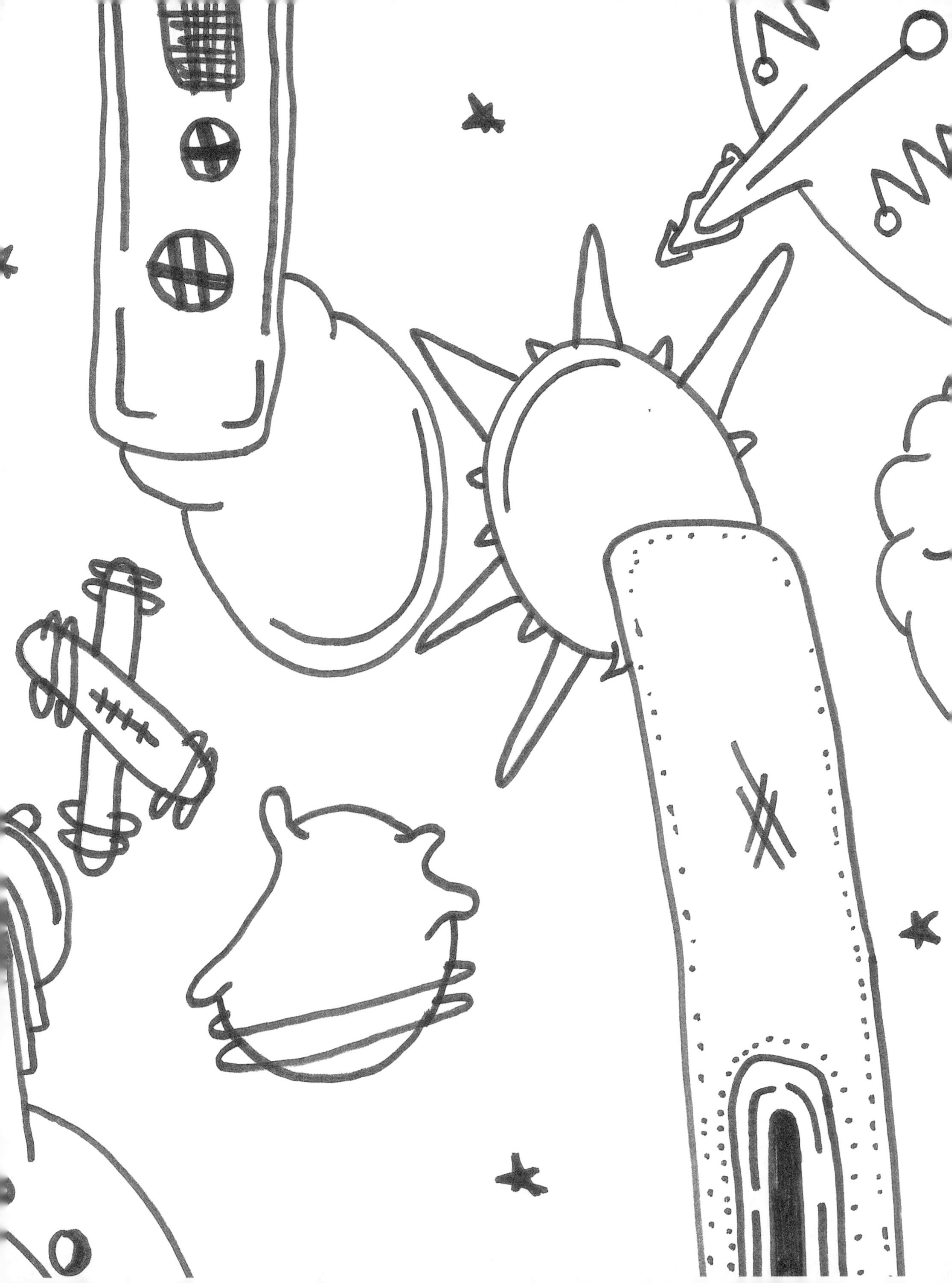

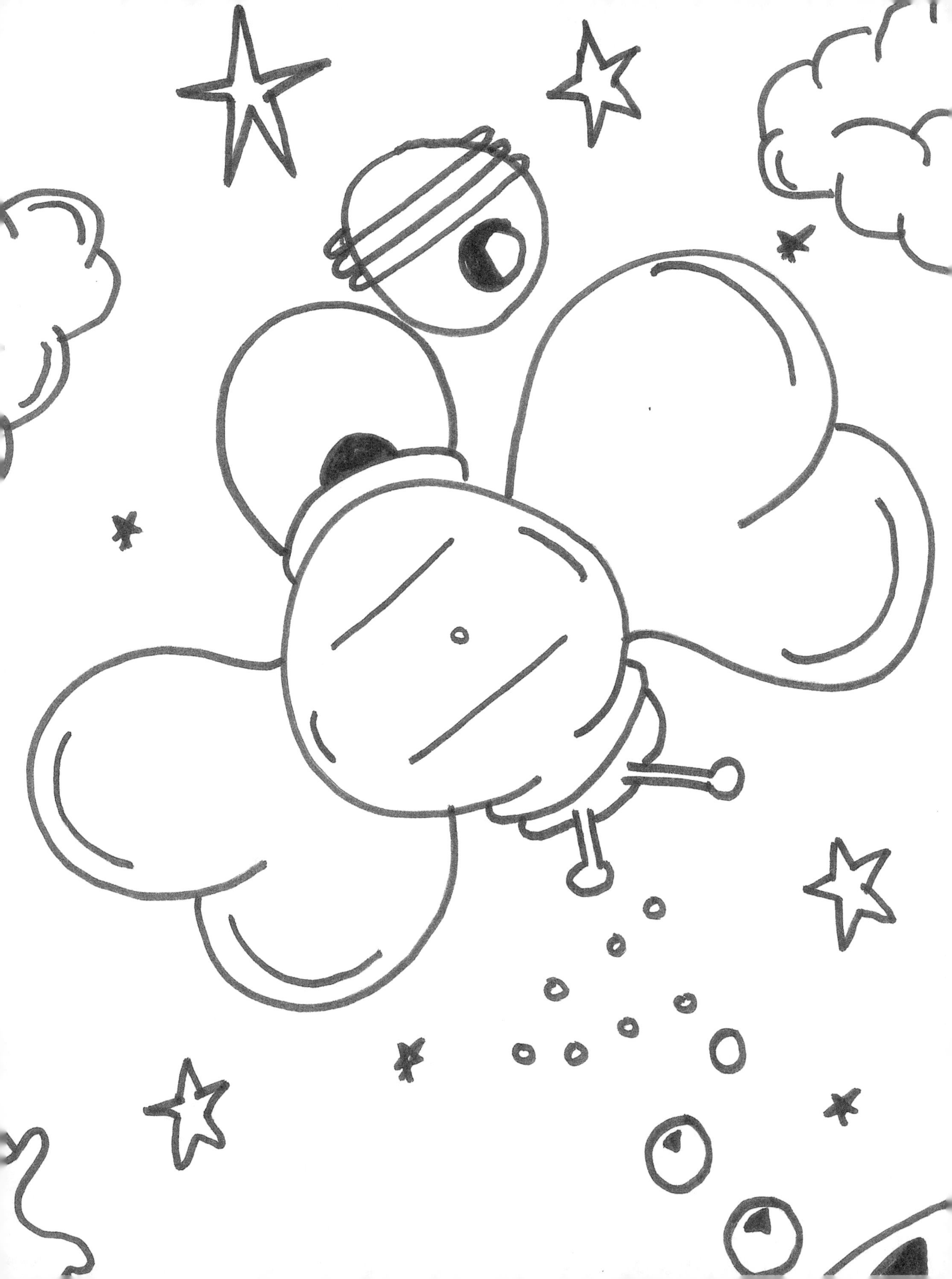

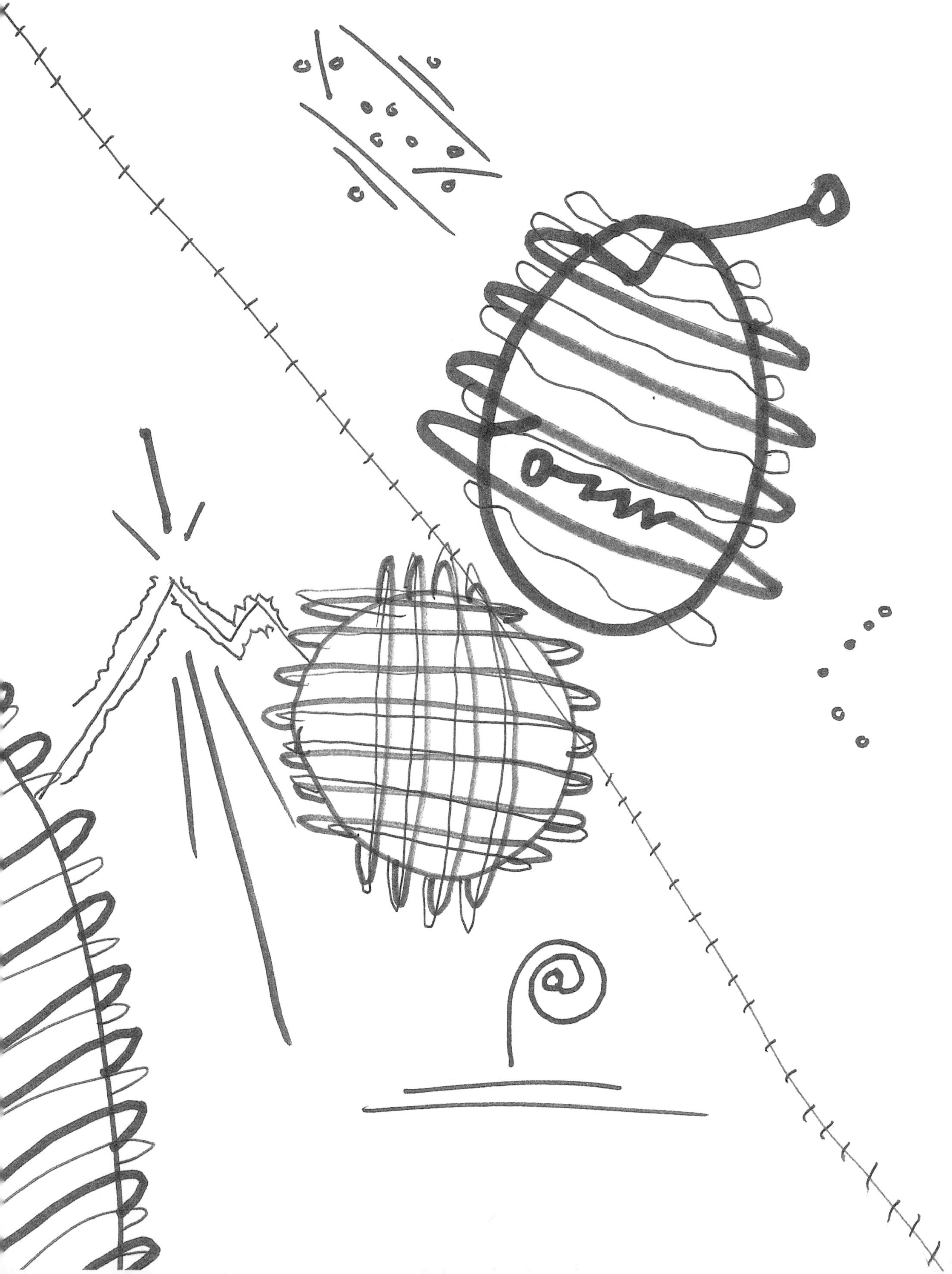

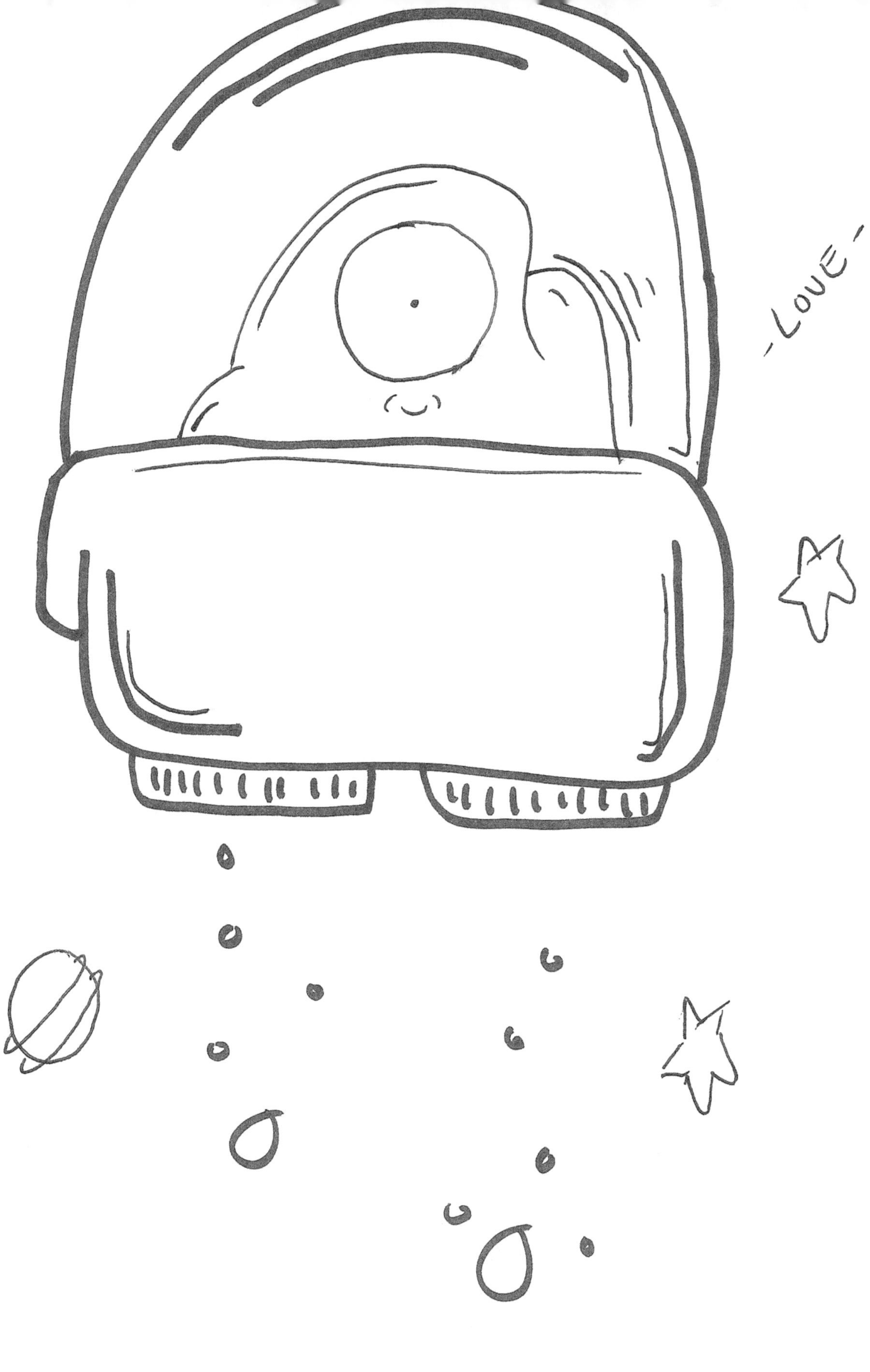
-LOVE-

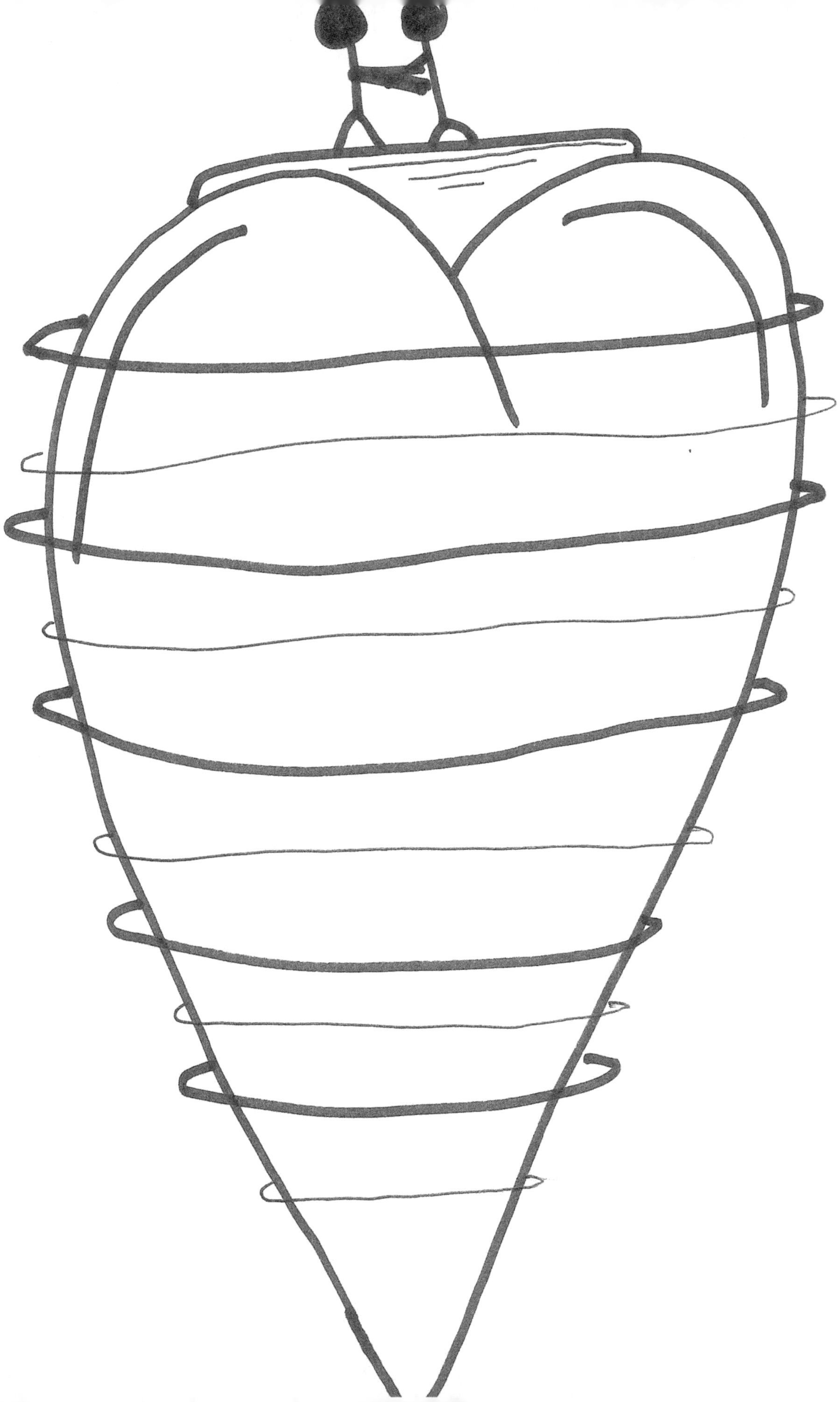

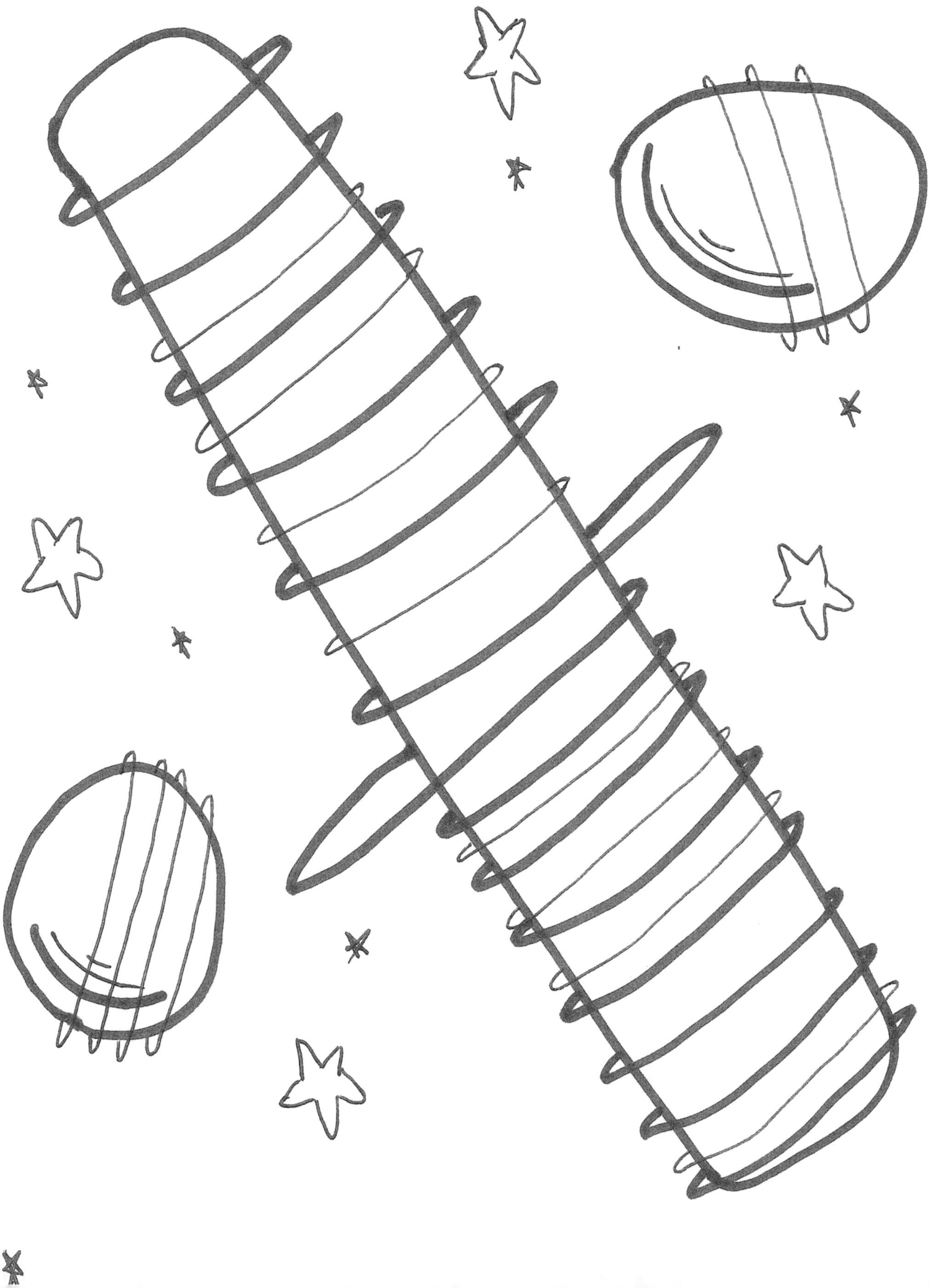

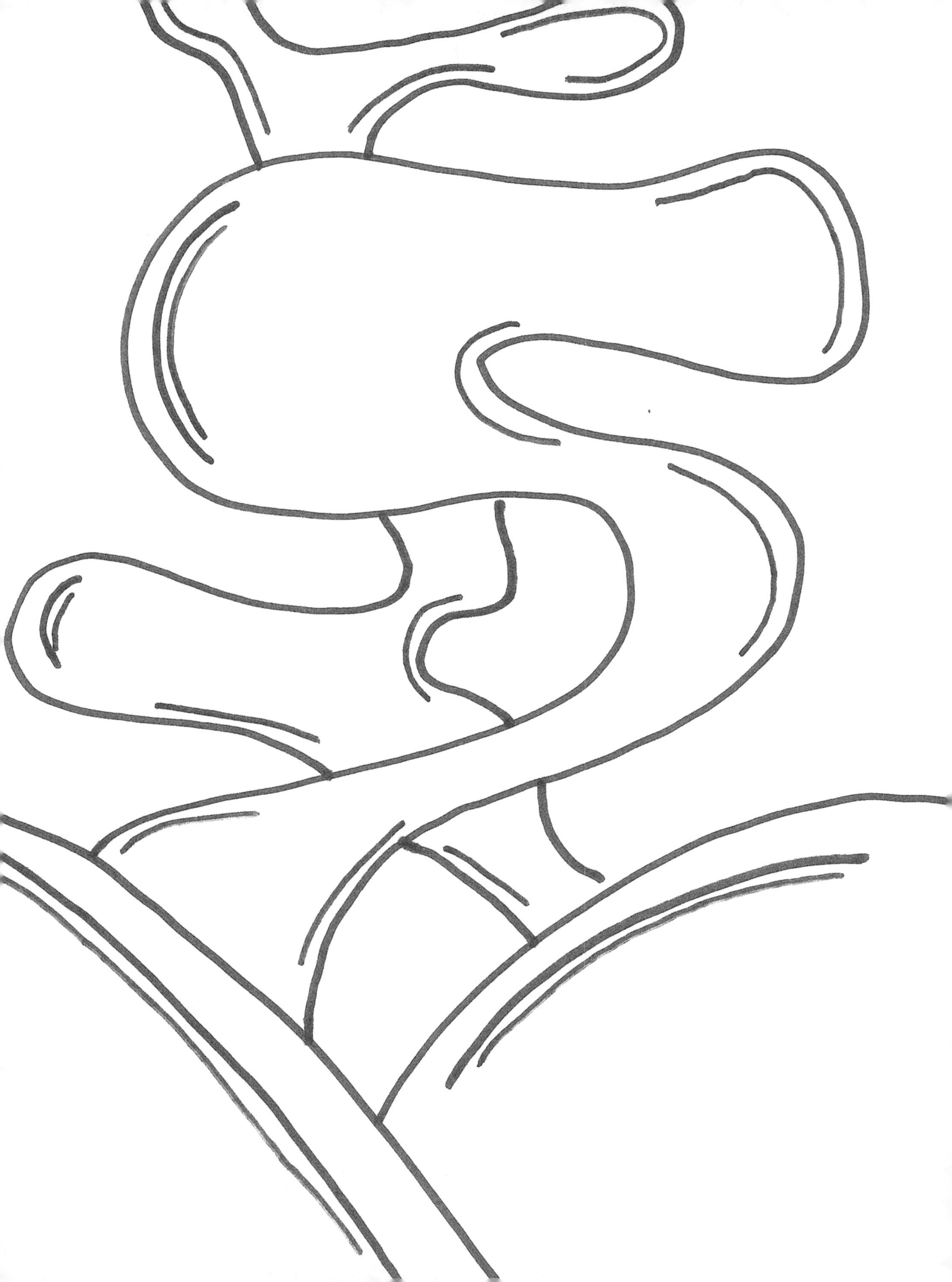

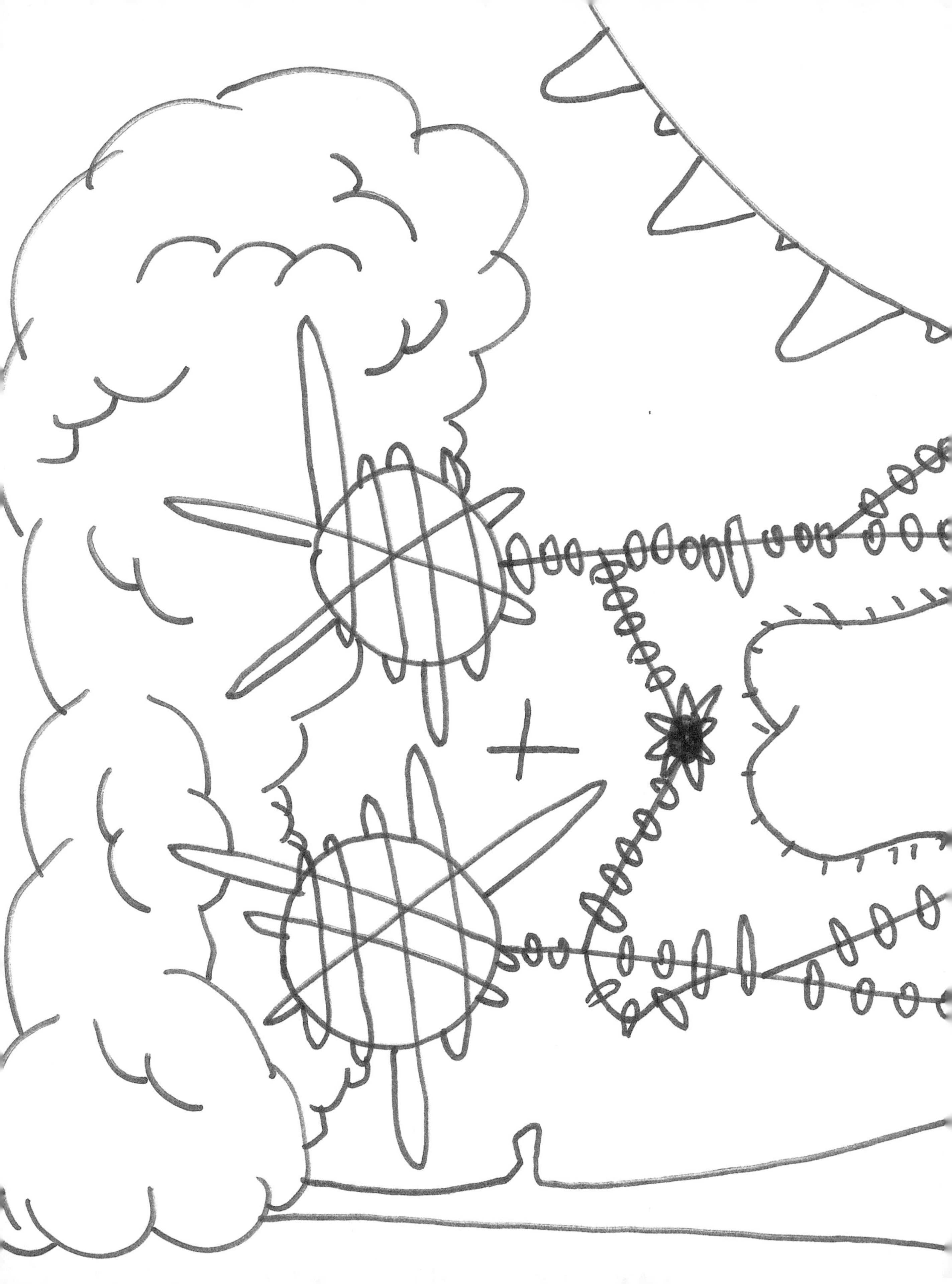

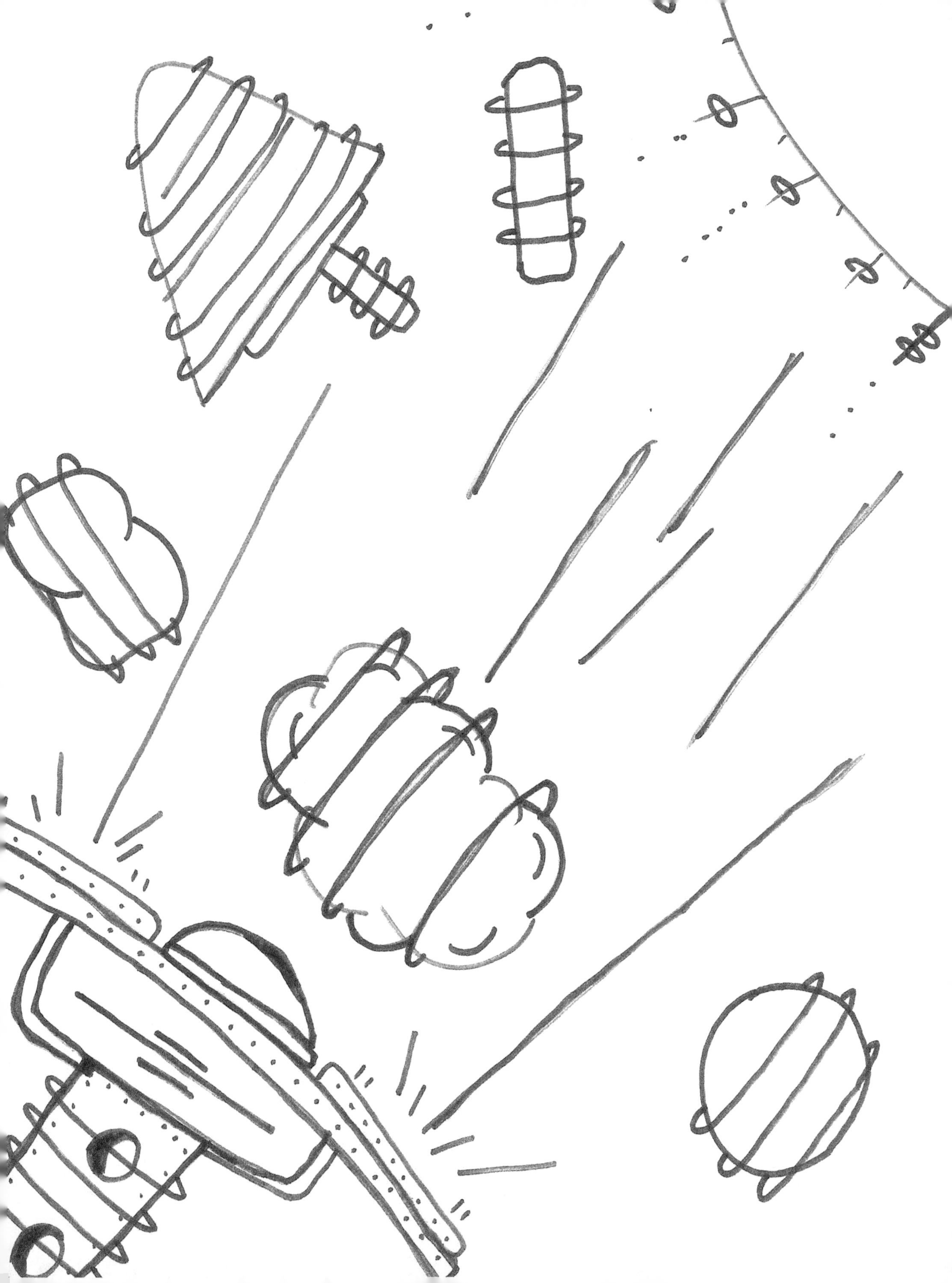

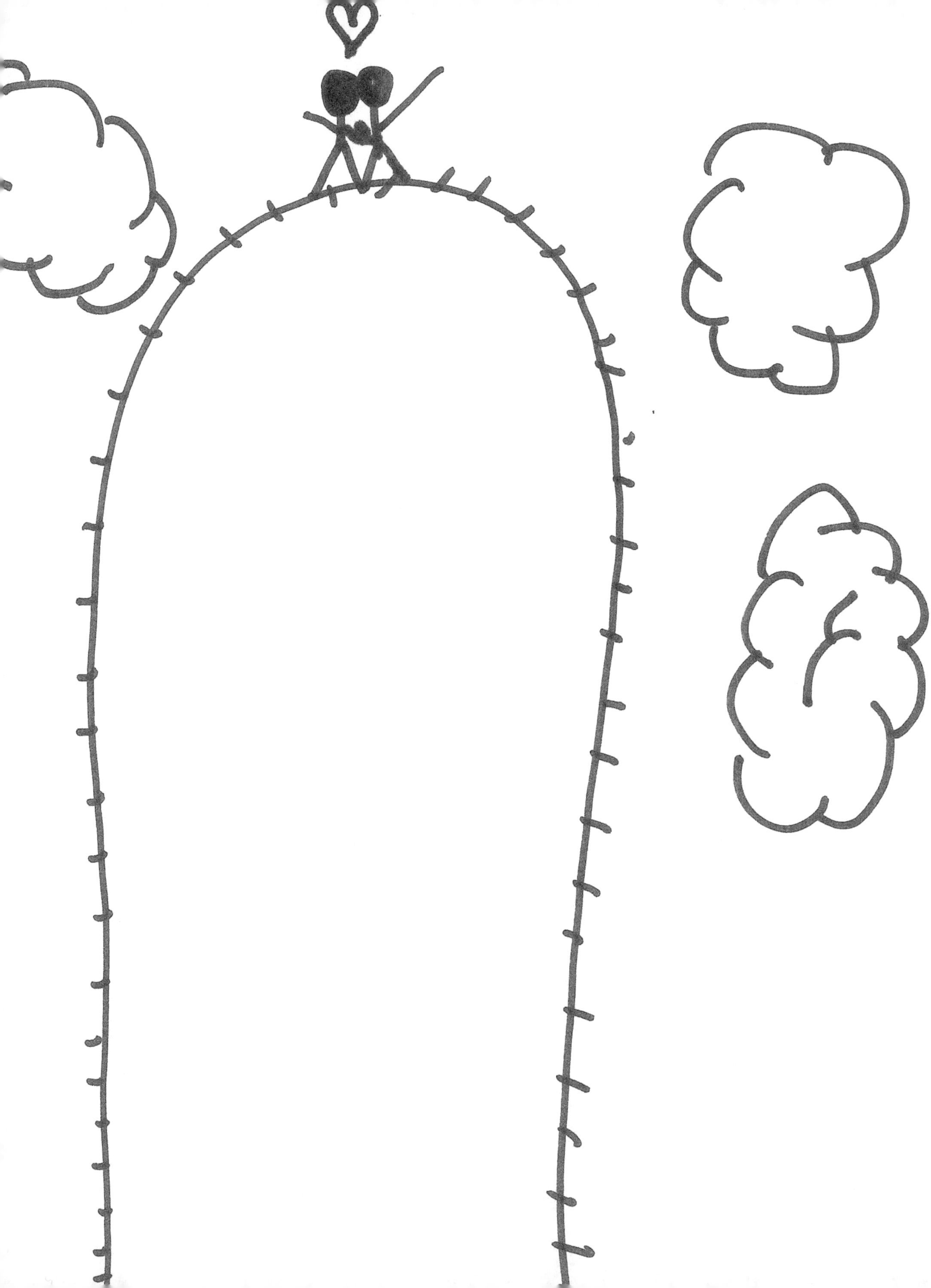

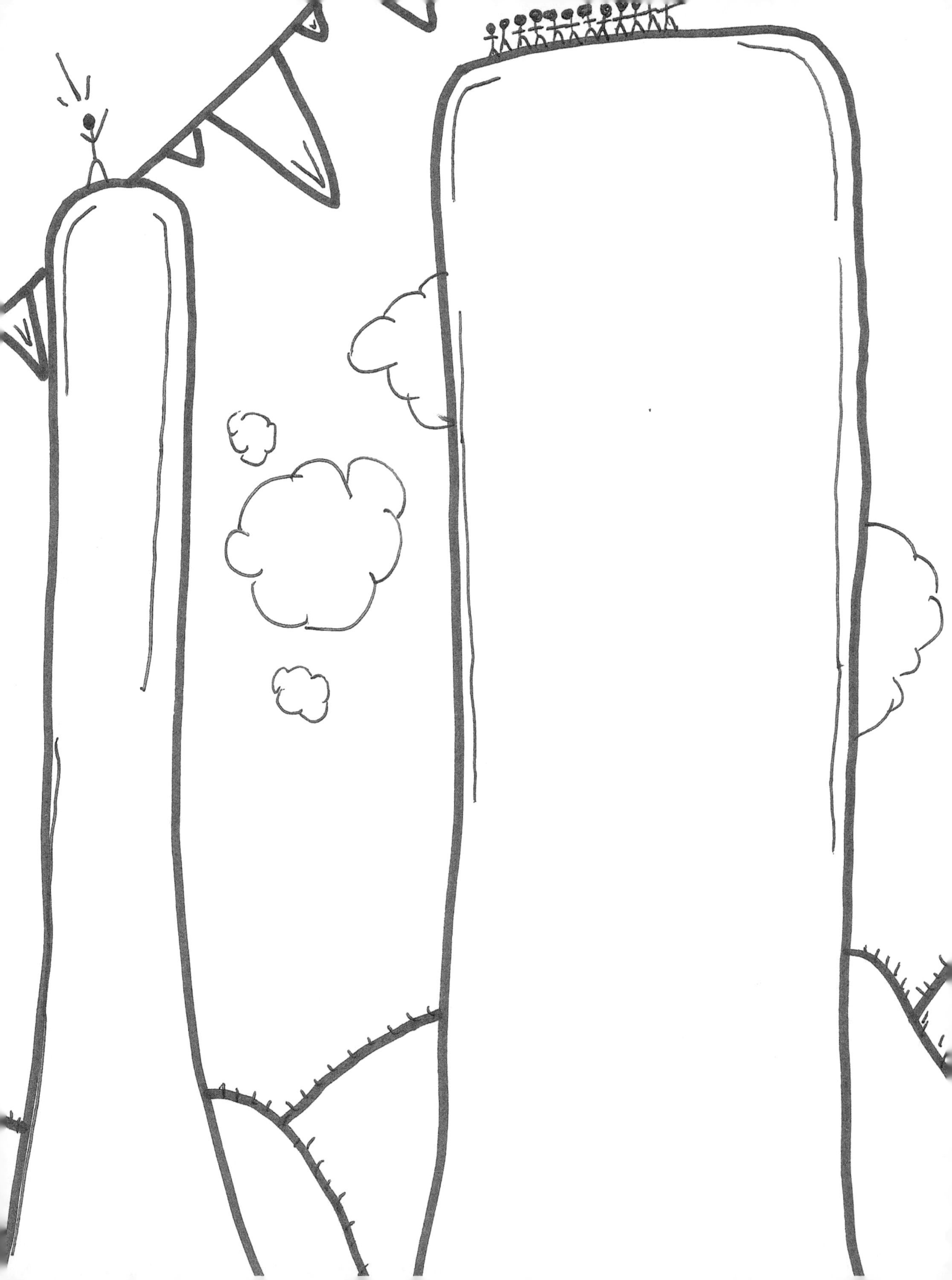

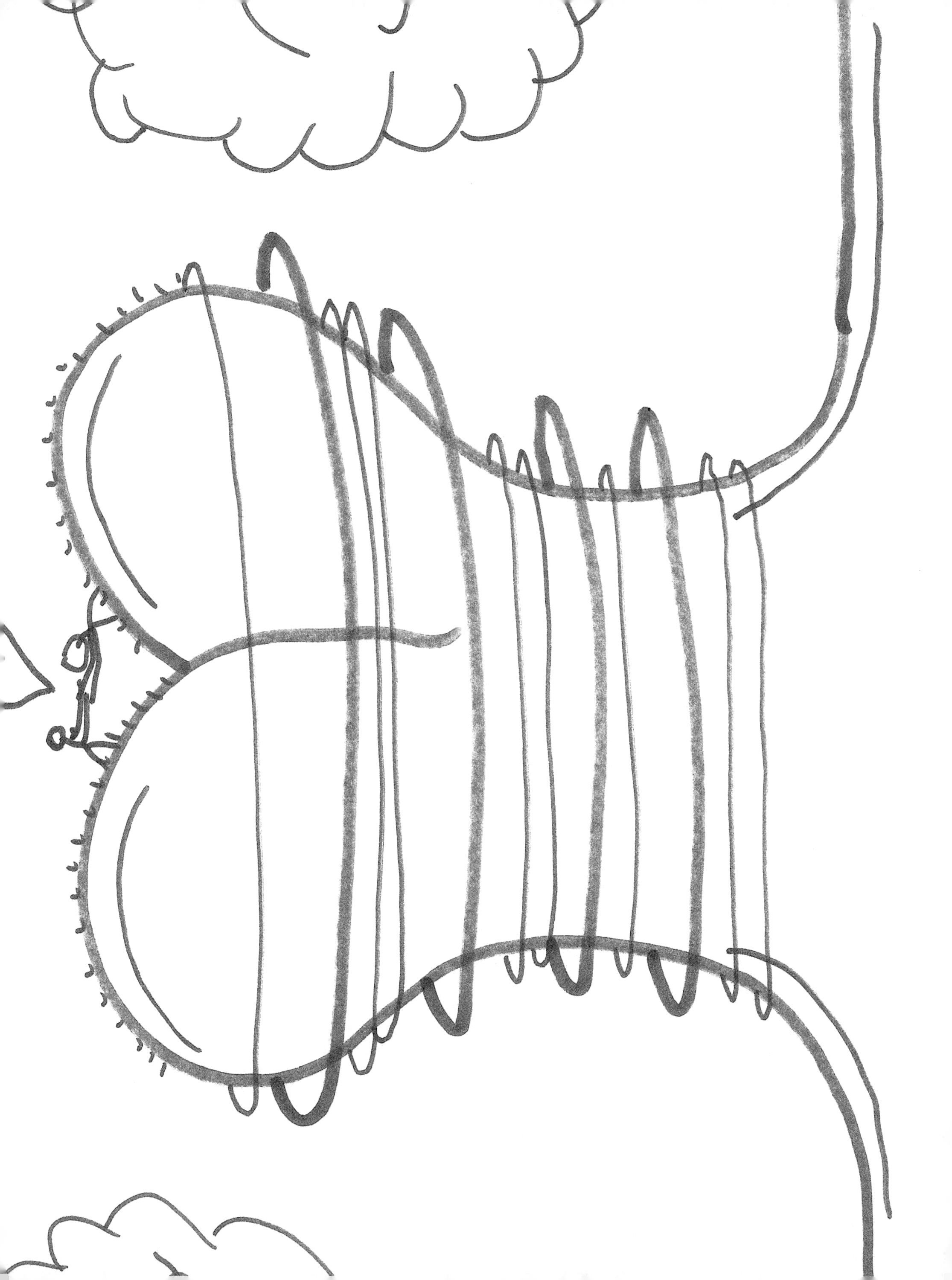

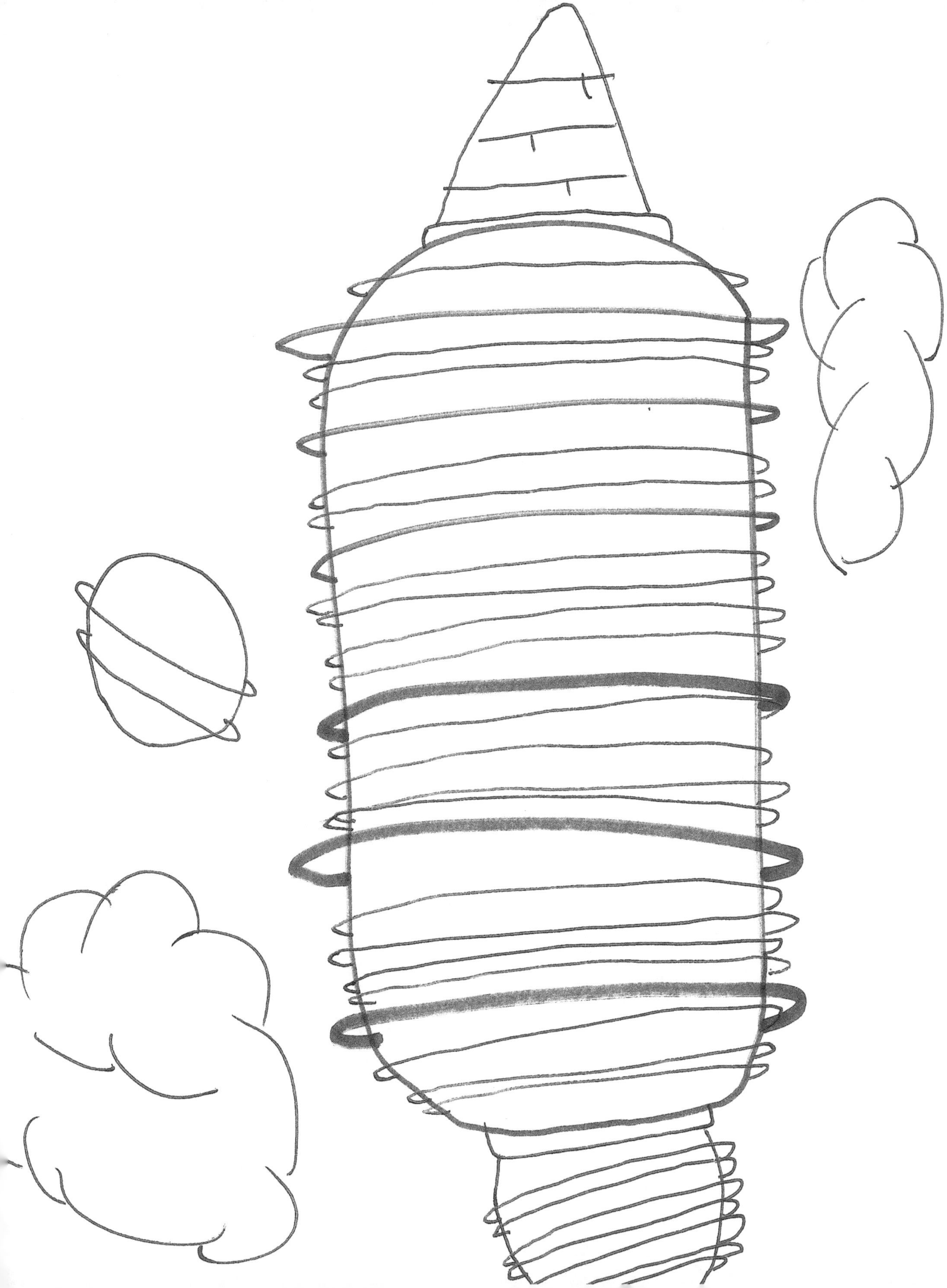

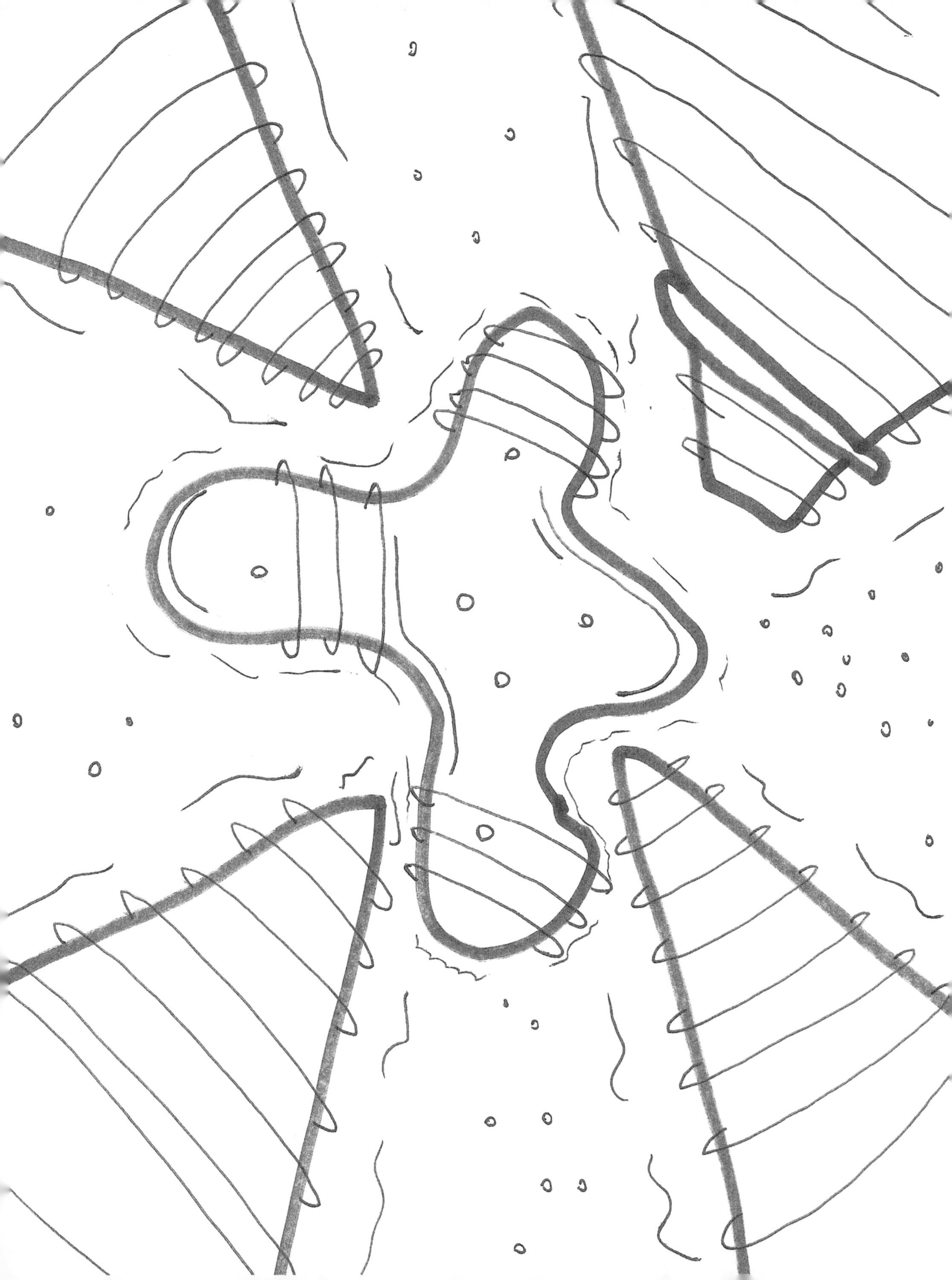

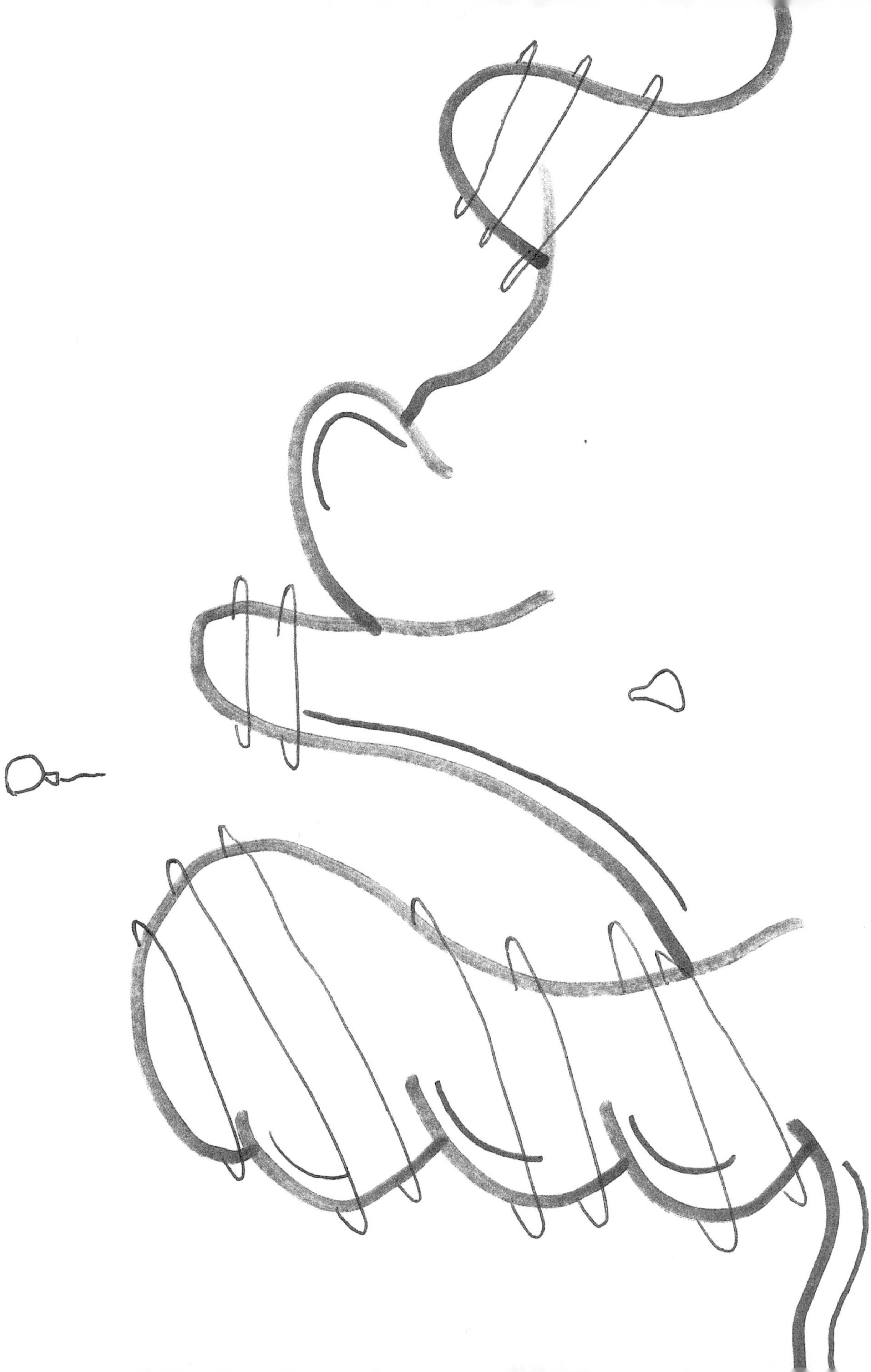

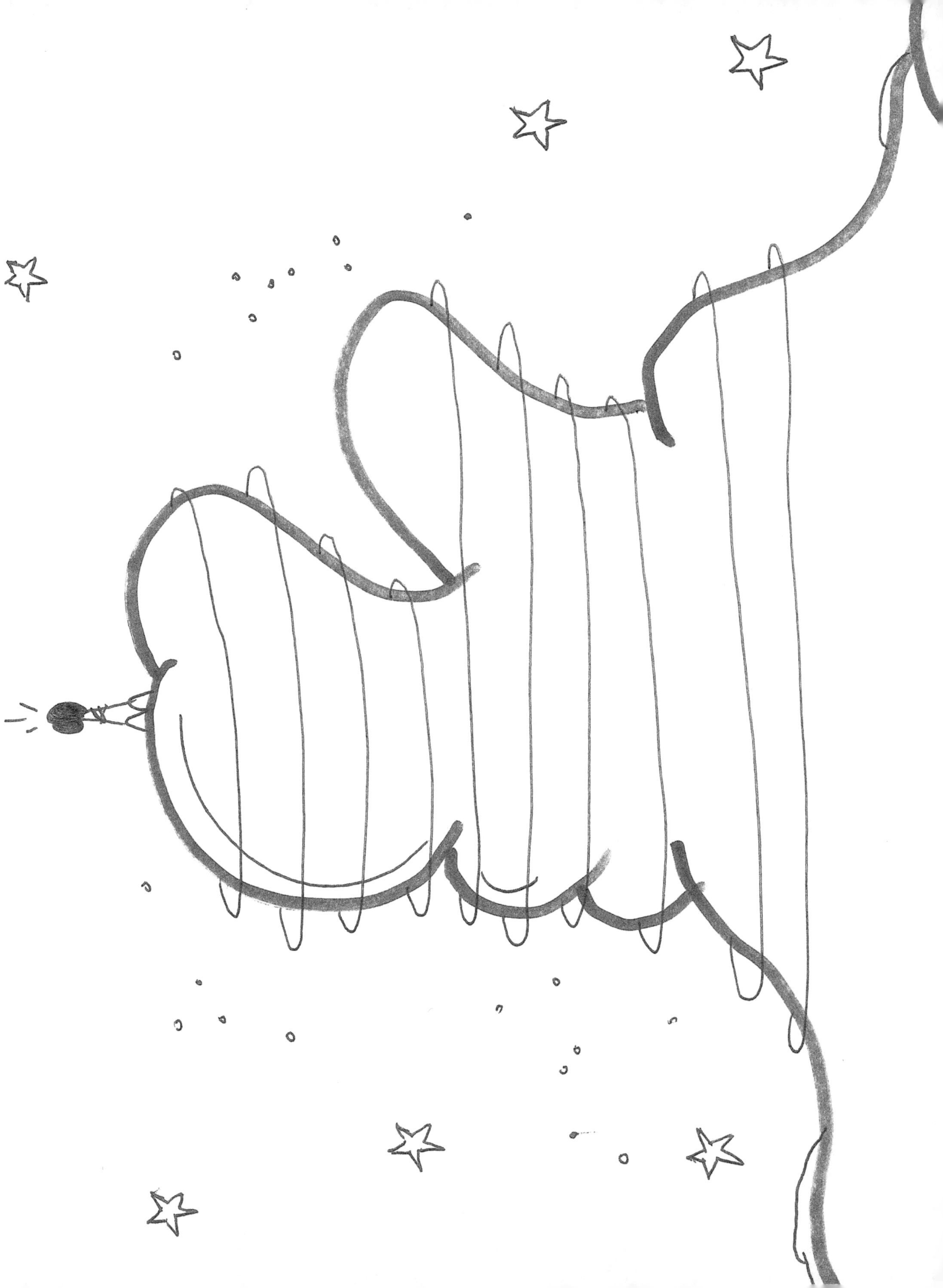

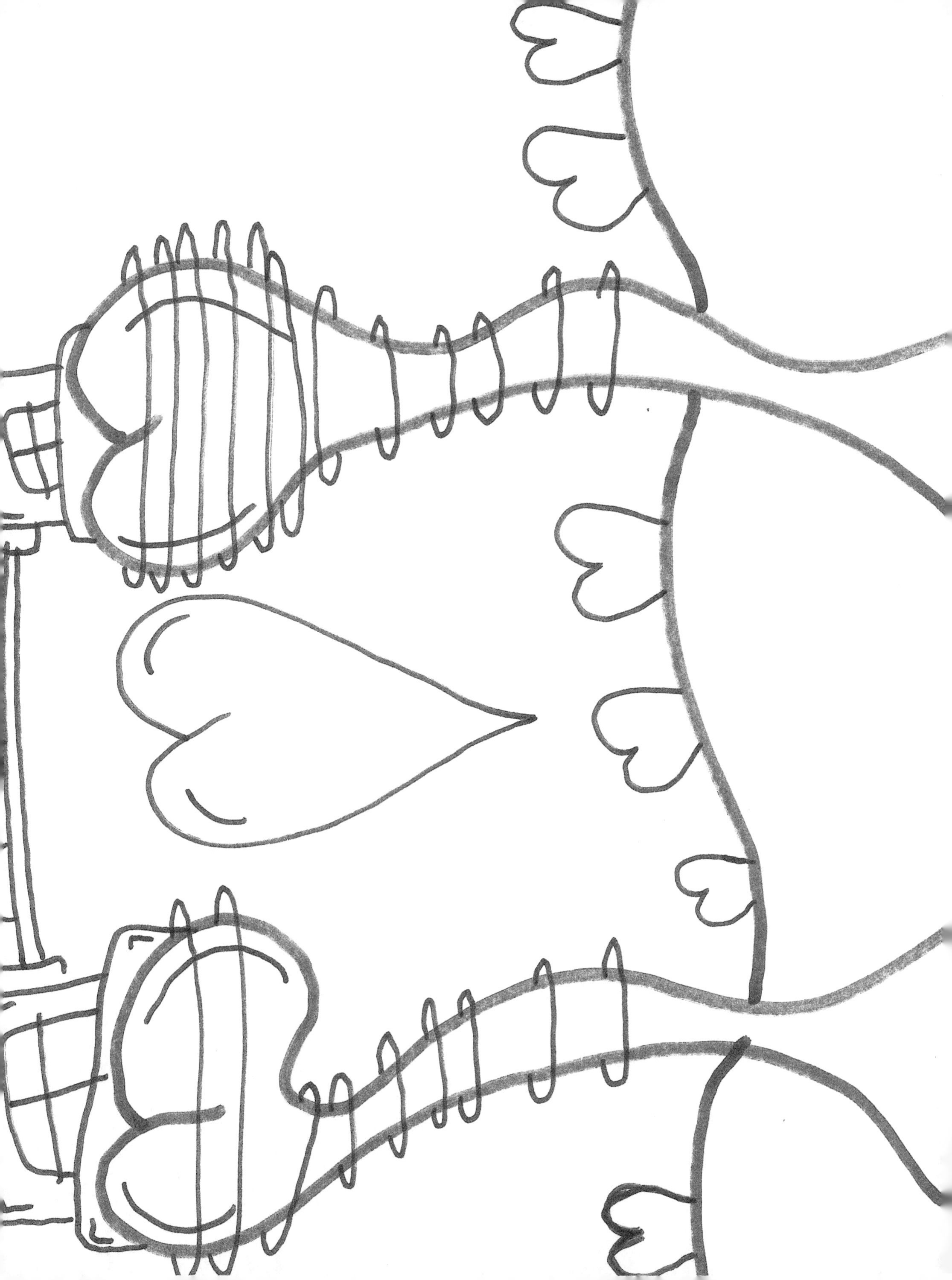

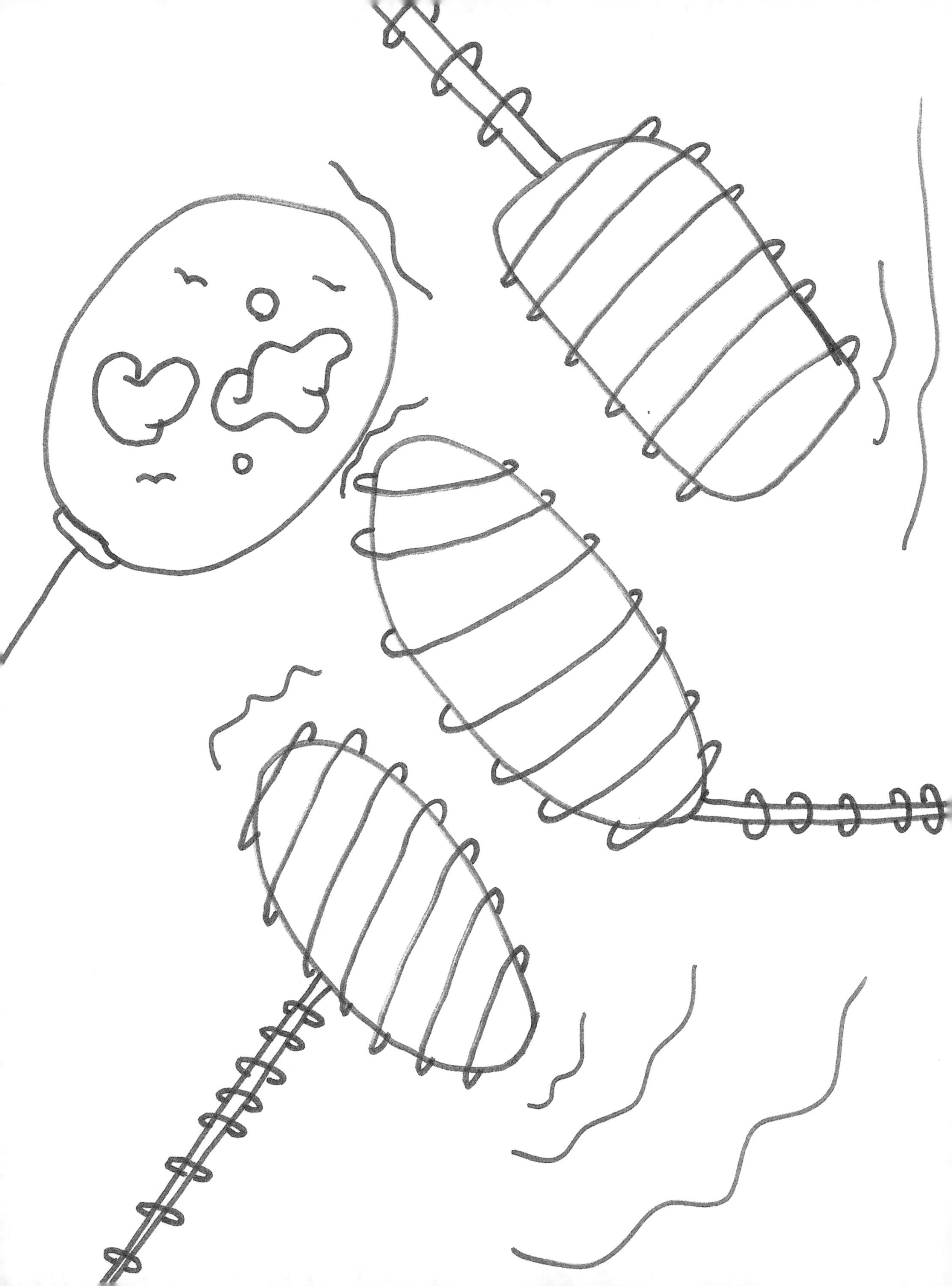

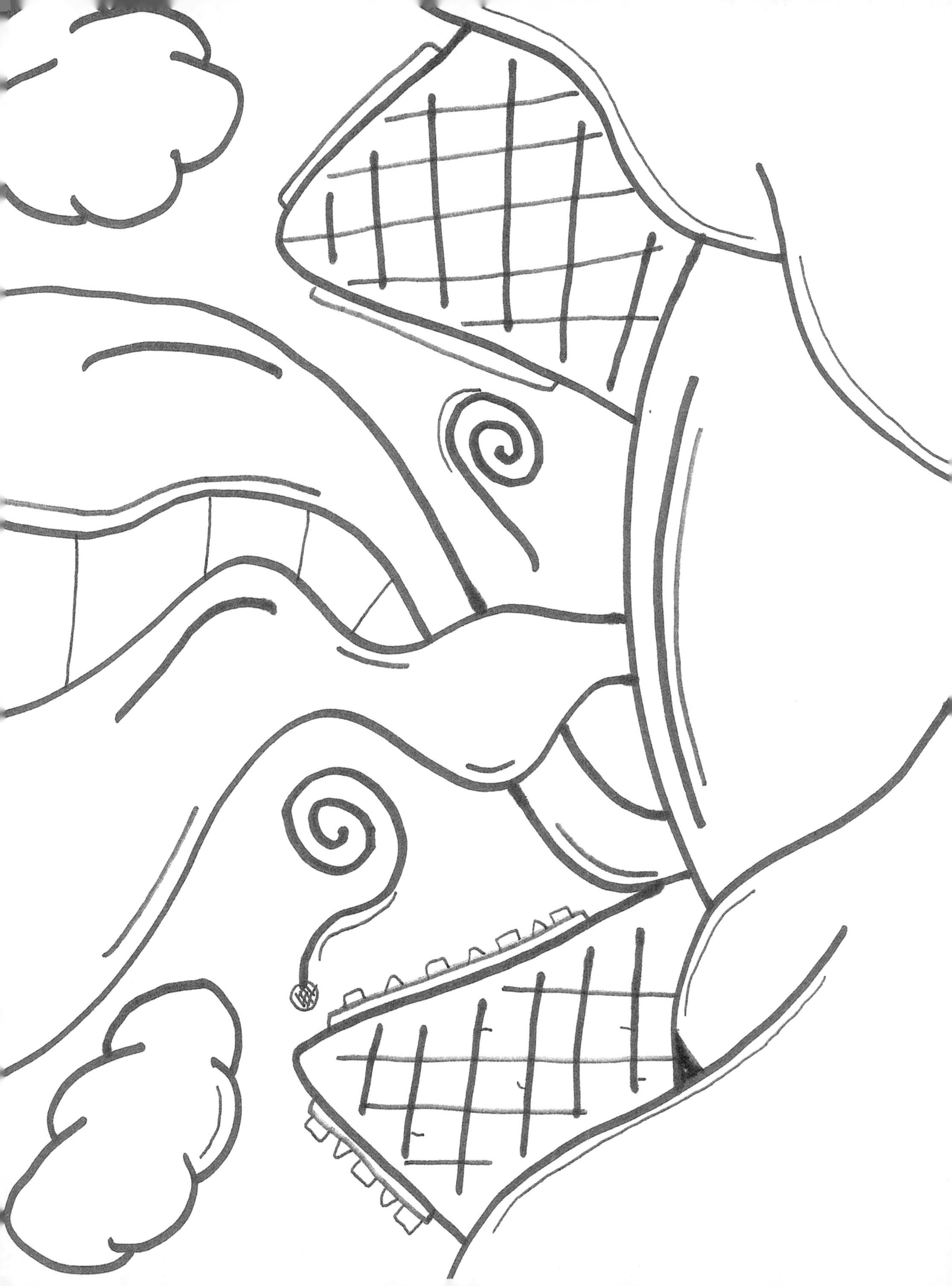

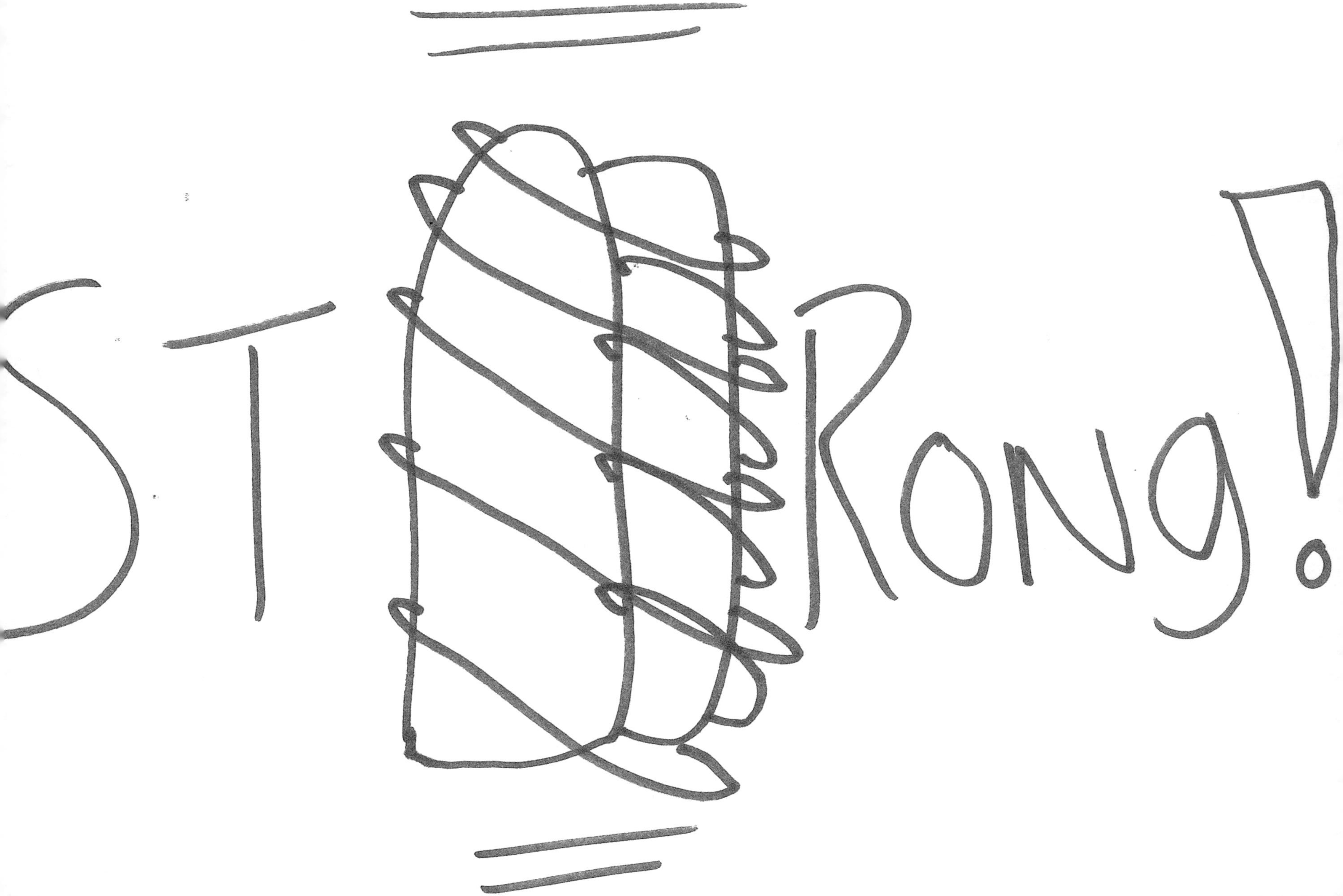
STRONG!

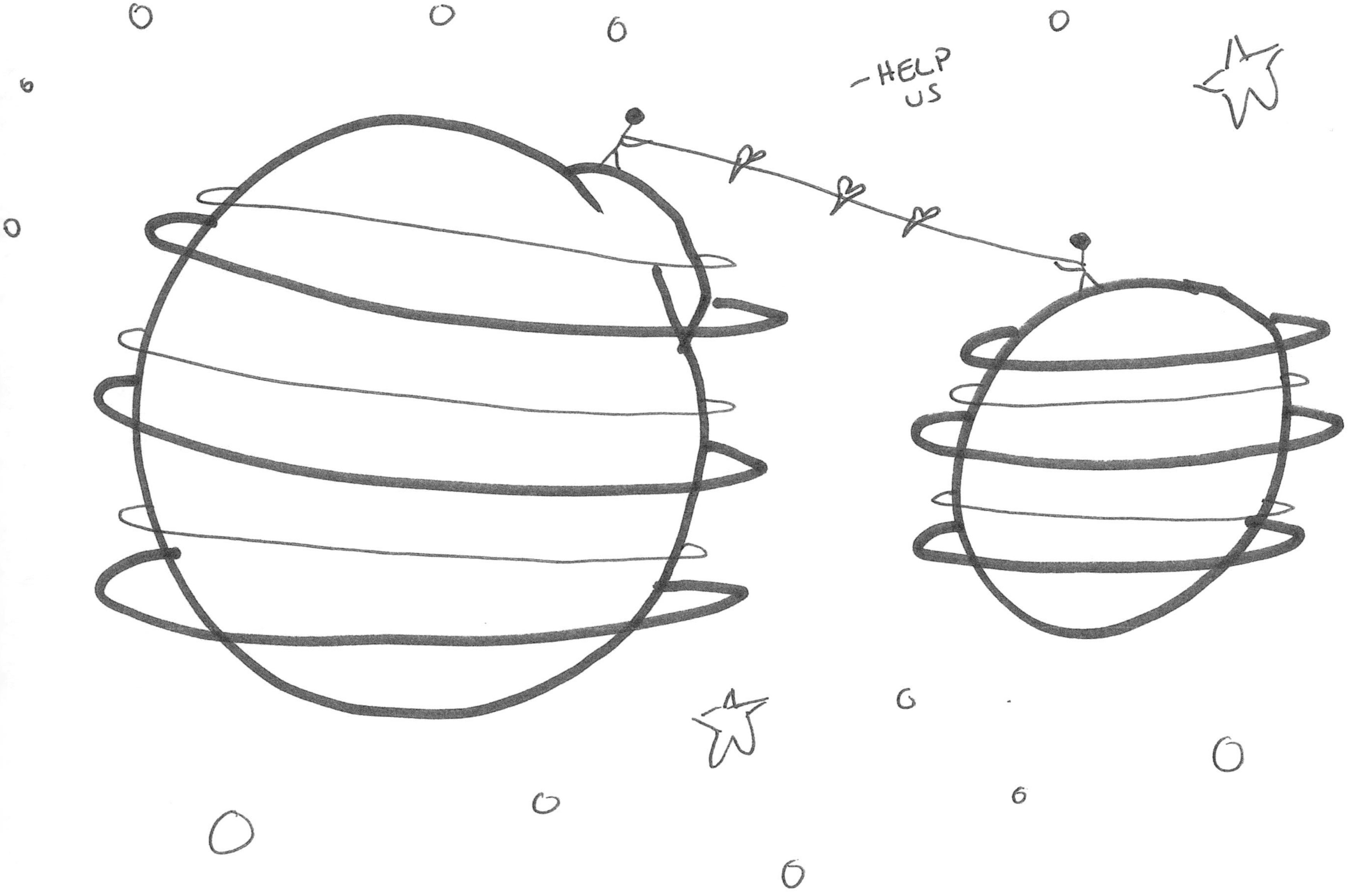
-HELP US

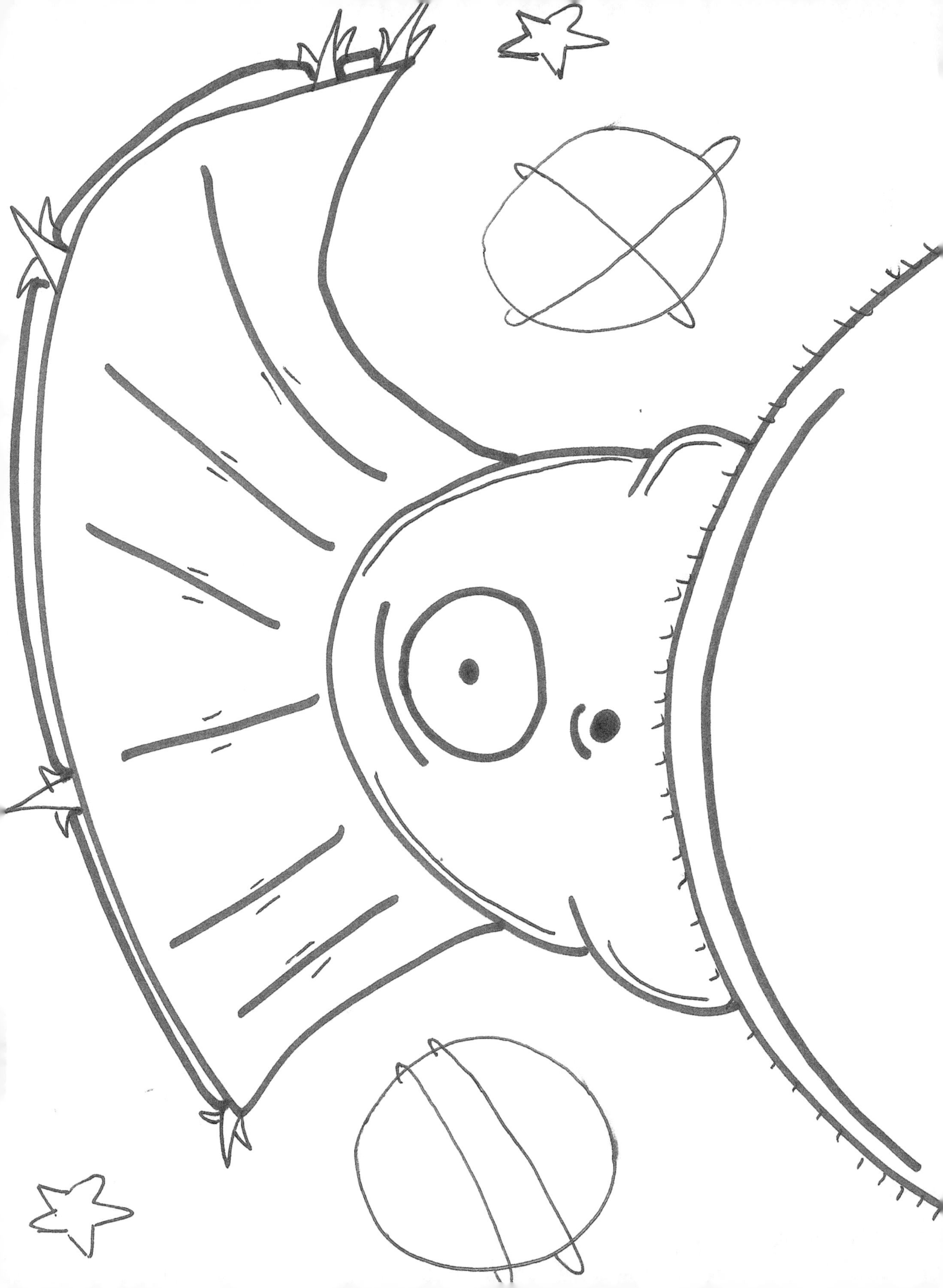

www.ingramcontent.com/pod-product-compliance
Lightning Source LLC
Chambersburg PA
CBHW080307180526
45167CB00006B/2708
* 9 7 8 1 4 9 4 8 4 3 9 6 0 *